I0893383

Praise for Bap

"A definitive theometry of Baphomet. Snuffin shows us exactly how and why this deity-form arose and developed into a major occult meme that has inspired many of the leading magicians, romantics, and rebels.... Impressive research and scholarship has gone into this book. If we define magic as the use of imaginary phenomena to create real effects, then the magical creation and evolution of the Baphomet concept has certainly had a profound effect on the ideas and actions of several generations.... Snuffin gradually reveals a deep personal relationship with Baphomet and provides practical meditations and rituals throughout."
—**PETER J. CARROLL**, renowned author and chaos magician

"Baphomet, a nuanced deity of paradox and evolution, is explored from every imaginable angle in this monumental book. Both academic and practical, Michael Osiris Snuffin's latest offering is invaluable for Pagans and occultists who are steadfastly devoted to exploring life's mysteries and finding our unique places in the world. This is the book we've been waiting for!"
—**RAVEN DIGITALIS**, author of *Esoteric Empathy*

"A deep dive into the enigmatic archetype of Baphomet, tracing its evolution from medieval conspiracy theories to modern Paganism and chaos magic. Exploring the origins of Baphomet in the trials of the Knights Templar, its iconic imagery as developed by occultist Éliphas Lévi, and its current role as a powerful symbol of nature, alchemy, and balance, this book offers readers a comprehensive understanding of this occult icon. Snuffin weaves history, ritual, and practical magic into a guide that reveals Baphomet's significance for modern spirituality, environmentalism, and personal transformation. This book provides essential insights into one of the most misunderstood and potent symbols in the world of magic."

—**JOHN J. COUGHLIN**, author of *Out of the Shadows*

"From the Templars to the Satanic Temple, from Lévi to LaVey, from Purgstall to Carroll, *Baphomet* plumbs the history, mystery, and lore surrounding its titular sphinx. Within these pages, Michael Osiris Snuffin traces Baphomet's evolution from the bogeyperson of past moral panics to a twenty-first-century figure embodying myriad interpretations in modern ritual."

—**RICHARD KACZYNSKI**, author of *Perdurabo: The Life of Aleister Crowley*

BAPHOMET

© Davin Mahi

About the Author

Michael Osiris Snuffin is a freelance editor and the author of *The Thoth Companion*. He has studied occultism for twenty-five years with an interest in Thelema, the Golden Dawn, chaos magic, and the Left-Hand Path (LHP). He is a former member of the Ordo Templi Orientis (O.T.O.) and founder of a Golden Dawn group. He is also a professional tarot reader. Visit him at Hermetic.com/osiris/index.

BAPHOMET

MICHAEL OSIRIS SNUFFIN

HISTORY, RITUAL & MAGIC OF THE WORLD'S MOST FAMOUS OCCULT ICON

LLEWELLYN
WOODBURY, MINNESOTA

First Edition
Second Printing, 2026

Book design by Rordan Brasington
Cover art by Tim Foley
Cover design by Kevin R. Brown
For a full list of art credits see page 241

Photography is used for illustrative purposes only. The persons depicted may not endorse or represent the book's subject.

Library of Congress Cataloging-in-Publication Data
Names: Snuffin, Michael Osiris, author.
Title: Baphomet : history, ritual & magic of the world's most famous occult icon / Michael Osiris Snuffin.
Description: First edition. | Woodbury, Minnesota : Llewellyn, [2025] | Includes bibliographical references. | Summary: "For Pagans who "seek to understand and work with Baphomet," a fascinating figure with a storied past. Contains historical information as well as testimonials from modern practitioners. Includes exercises and meditations"-- Provided by publisher.
Identifiers: LCCN 2024058951 (print) | LCCN 2024058952 (ebook) | ISBN 9780738778310 (paperback) | ISBN 9780738778334 (ebook)
Subjects: LCSH: Baphomet (Legendary character) | Magic. | Ritual.
Classification: LCC BF1556 .S67 2025 (print) | LCC BF1556 (ebook) | DDC 133.4/3--dc23/eng/20250122
LC record available at https://lccn.loc.gov/2024058951
LC ebook record available at https://lccn.loc.gov/2024058952

Llewellyn Publications
A Division of Llewellyn Worldwide Ltd.
2143 Wooddale Drive
Woodbury, MN 55125-2989
www.llewellyn.com

Printed in the United States of America

GPSR Representation:
UPI-2M PLUS d.o.o., Medulićeva 20, 10000 Zagreb, Croatia
matt.parsons@upi2mbooks.hr

Other Books by Michael Osiris Snuffin

The Thoth Companion: The Key to the True Symbolic Meaning of the Thoth Tarot

The Complete Conjuring Spirits: A Manual of Modern Sorcery

Introduction to Romantic Satanism

Acknowledgments

Many thanks to everyone who assisted and supported me during the creation of this book. Two people were particularly helpful.

Miranda Anderson became my friend around the time I started working on this book. She has been my sounding board for the project over the last few years, offering useful support and advice when needed. Miranda also read the first draft of the manuscript and offered many suggestions, including convincing me to remove a chapter from the book that really didn't belong.

I became friends with Raven Digitalis in September of 2022 when he came to Tacoma to promote *The Empath's Oracle*. Raven has been an ardent supporter of this book, and he helped me negotiate some of the complexities of submitting the manuscript to Llewellyn. His aid was particularly valuable after I had a brain tumor removed (which was thankfully benign) in October of 2023, when I needed a little extra help getting my manuscript ready for publication.

Miranda and Raven, I am eternally grateful for your help! Thank you.

Contents

SOLVE
COAGULA
ELIPHAS
LEVI DEL.

Foreword

The first time I saw Éliphas Lévi's well-known drawing of Baphomet I was about ten years old. It was in a big thick book about witchcraft and demonology that I somehow stumbled across in the library. I knew, even at a young age, that this figure had some kind of deep esoteric meaning, although I had no idea what it might be. I wasn't old enough to comprehend the content of that text, but that didn't stop me from borrowing the same book again and again to look at the picture and wonder. This powerful image spoke to me in a way I couldn't explain. It contained secrets. It was fascinating and maybe a little frightening. It has stuck with me my whole life, and I feel the same way about it all these years later. However, I have always had more questions than answers about the enigma that is Baphomet.

When I heard through the grapevine recently that there was going to be a book released all about this compelling being, I was excited and extremely curious. After all, I have struggled to find and understand much of the material that exists about Baphomet. Those old occult texts are sometimes a tough read.

I had high hopes for Michael Osiris Snuffin's *Baphomet: History, Ritual & Magic of the Word's Most Famous Occult Icon* and was not disappointed.

Snuffin has a wealth of occult knowledge that can only be attributed to lifelong passion and curiosity. This is evidenced by his previous works about the Thoth tarot, Goetic and Enochian sorcery, and (of particular interest to me) Romantic Satanism. It can't be overstated just how much dedication and time has gone into fully comprehending these complex subjects, something Snuffin has decoded for the reader so that we, too, can understand. *Baphomet* takes an academic and historically informed approach to an often-misunderstood icon, providing context and perspectives from various key practitioners who helped shape its development. The author has provided original ritual structures from various sources and presented some of their own as well. In the end, we are left with a concise index of information from which to build an understanding of Baphomet, what they are and why, and the knowledge that they can be incorporated into many existing spiritual practices.

If you're reading this book, it's likely you already know that Baphomet is more than just a so-called evil being. If you've attempted to research them, you may, like me, have encountered a tangled labyrinth of information that seems impossible to solve. The history of such a powerful image is naturally complicated and lengthy. Snuffin helps the reader traverse this in an organized and unbiased way.

This book also happens to be timely. Interestingly, Baphomet seems to be hovering in the collective unconscious these days. We're seeing images of them pop up again and again in unexpected places, like a symbol—or dare I say, an omen. They're on television shows, included in political demonstrations, and even stylized into cute stuffed toys. One has to wonder: Why is such a meaningful symbol being shown to us with such frequency, and why today?

Perhaps Baphomet as the representative of the union of opposites is here to remind us of the true balance of the universe and planet in turbulent times.

Faster than ever before in human history, we are individually and collectively experiencing destruction and rebirth, growth and shedding,constant change. Baphomet symbolizes this intense time-lapse as we careen toward a seemingly chaotic fate while reminding us that destruction is always paired with its opposite, creation. From this, we can perceive that we are all part of something much larger and there is more to the picture of our lives and the universe than we know.

Snuffin has encapsulated Baphomet's multifaceted spirit within this book. You might begin with only a scattered understanding of Baphomet, but you will emerge with a cohesive and enlightened perspective.

—Kate Freuler, author of *Magic at the Crossroads: The Devil in Modern Witchcraft* (Llewellyn, 2024) and *Of Blood and Bones: Working with Shadow Magick and the Dark Moon* (Llewellyn, 2020)

SOLVE
COAGULA

Introduction

I first encountered the esoteric Baphomet more than twenty-five years ago while studying the works of Éliphas Lévi and Aleister Crowley. Like many Pagan practitioners, I was fascinated by Lévi's famous image of Baphomet first published in *Doctrine and Ritual of High Magic* (1856), wondering what the icon truly represented and what secrets might be hidden within. Over the years, my interest in Baphomet continued to grow, but I found little information on Baphomet as an esoteric deity. Unlike most other Pagan deities, there is no mythology to draw upon to define Their personality or reveal Their powers. Baphomet was an esoteric enigma to me.

I wrote this book to answer two questions: Who is the divine Baphomet, and why would you want to work with Them? After five years of research and personal work with the deity, I have determined that Baphomet is the divine egregore of the life-force of the biosphere of planet Earth, a deity first described by Chaos magician Peter Carroll in

Liber Null & Psychonaut (1987). Baphomet is primarily associated with nature, the five elements, alchemy, and sexuality.

I also had a third question, a seemingly simple one that would turn out to reveal the true purpose of Baphomet. As the egregore of the life-force of the Earth, Baphomet came into being when life on this planet came into being a few billion years ago. So why did They wait to fully reveal Themselves to humanity until the mid-nineteenth century? Because that is when humans started doing large-scale damage to the planet's ecosystem. Industrialization, urbanization, and advancements in agriculture, sanitation, and medicine during the nineteenth century led to a dramatic increase in the number of humans, and the large-scale damage that we inflicted on the environment led to the endangerment and extinction of many other forms of life. This ecological destruction continues to disturb the balance of our biosphere and Baphomet.

Baphomet is very sensitive to the ebb and flow of life-energy on this planet, and the threat to our natural ecosystem became so dire that Baphomet chose to reveal Themselves to humanity, seeking to influence us to change our ways of living. Baphomet is also disturbed by the acceleration of climate change in the last two hundred years as it threatens to destroy even more life forms on the planet, including the humans that created the problem. We need to change our ways, and Baphomet has come forth to help.

About This Book

This book consists of three parts. In part one, I examine the evolution of Baphomet from a mysterious name to a spiritual entity. I explain how Baphomet was conceived during the trial of the Templars, created by Éliphas Lévi to serve as an icon of the magic and alchemy, and deified in the works of Aleister Crowley. I also look at how modern nontheistic Satanic perspectives of Baphomet have affected esoteric and public perceptions of Baphomet.

Part two looks at the proliferation of Baphomet as a Pagan deity in the late twentieth and early twenty-first centuries, focusing on how Pagan practitioners identify and interact with Them. I start by examining Peter Carroll's reconception of Baphomet and how it has been expounded upon by other Chaos Magicians. I then investigate two other Pagan conceptions of the deity: a Baphomet Rite performed at an Australian Pagan festival and an experiential conception of Baphomet revealed by devotees Raven Kaldera and Ruth Addams.

Part three takes the conceptions of Baphomet from parts one and two and uses them to create a composite picture of Baphomet that defines Them and what They can do. I provide practical methods of contacting and working with Baphomet using meditation and ritual. Part three introduces a process called Elemental Alchemy, which gives instructions on how to begin to rectify our disconnection with nature in order to heal ourselves and in turn learn to live harmoniously with the planet.

Final Words

Before I reveal the mysteries of Baphomet, here are a few final notes. Among other things, the figure of Baphomet represents the entire spectrum of gender identity and gender expression. For this reason, I use They/Them/Their pronouns when referring to Baphomet, capitalized because they refer to a deity. Unfortunately, many of the authors I quote from use gendered pronouns for Baphomet, their books having been written before the use of they/them pronouns became more widespread and acceptable. I apologize in advance for the confusion that sometimes arises from this linguistic conflict.

The name Baphomet may be pronounced BAH-FO-MAY (French) or BAF-O-MET (English); both are correct, so use whichever one works for you. However, in group ritual, it does sound more harmonious if everyone uses the same pronunciation.

Michael Osiris Snuffin, 2024

SOLVE ET COAGULA

PART ONE

HISTORY

Chapter 1

The Templar-Mason Conspiracy

The conception of Baphomet begins with the destruction of the Knights Templar, for the trial of the Templars is the first place we learn about the mysterious Baphomet. While the Templars were accused of many heretical acts, the most bizarre charge leveled against them was that they worshiped heads or idols of a demon called Baphomet. While no evidence of this devil worship was ever found, the allegations endured.

When the mystical fraternal order known as the Freemasons declared that they were the descendants of the Templars, their detractors and enemies sought to discredit them by connecting the Masons with the heresy of the Templars and the worship of Baphomet. When the Catholic Church, threatened by Masonic ideals like individual liberty and religious pluralism, condemned the Masons for conspiring to destroy the church in the nineteenth century, Baphomet appeared as proof of Satanism within the Masonic order. The problem was that none of it was true.

Holy Knights

In the last part of the eleventh century, the Byzantine Empire lost control of Jerusalem and other Christian holy sites in a string of military defeats by the Muslim Turks. This sparked the First Crusade (1095–1099), a European military campaign that liberated the Holy Land from the Muslims, culminating in the recapture of Jerusalem and the establishment of the Crusader states.

In Jerusalem circa 1119, nine knights led by Hughes de Payens took vows of poverty and chastity, and swore obedience to the Patriarch of Jerusalem, Baldwin II. They took up the protection of pilgrims in the Holy Land as their sacred cause. Baldwin granted the knights lodging in the palace stables, located on the site of the original Temple of Solomon; thus this small order of knights became known as the Poor Knights of the Temple of Solomon, or simply the Knights Templar.

This small group of knights came to the attention of Bernard of Clairvaux, a popular and influential abbot who took special interest in the idea of a monastic military order. At the Council of Troyes in 1128, called at Bernard's insistence, the Knights Templar gained official recognition by the church under Pope Honorius II. Officially known as the Poor Fellow-Soldiers of Christ and the Temple of Solomon, the Templars had their own priests and bishops and answered to the Pope alone.

The Seal of the Knights Templar

The church provided the Templars with the Templar Rule, a strict monastic code of conduct based on the Benedictine Rule. Like other monks, Templars took vows of poverty and celibacy; wore simple clothes; and ate, slept, and prayed together. However, there were also exceptions and additional rules to accommodate the need to maintain a battle-ready army of knights. They could not fast in the traditional manner, as it would weaken the soldiers; they could eat meat three times a week to maintain their strength; and most importantly, while men consecrated to God could not shed blood, the Templars got a special dispensation from the Pope to slay the enemies of Christianity.

The Templars grew quickly and soon amassed a great deal of wealth. The knights took vows of poverty and gave all their assets to the Templars upon joining. The Templars also received many donations of wealth and property from enthusiastic European nobles and lords, who lacked the resources to send their own soldiers on expensive military campaigns in the Holy Land and who sought dispensations from the church. The farms, mills, and other industries granted to the Templars often produced commercial goods and turned a profit. Known for their financial acumen, the Templars started managing estates of nobles in France and other countries, later even serving as tax collectors.

The Templars needed this wealth to pay for their expensive military campaigns in the Holy Land. They developed a large transportation network to move men and supplies by land and by sea from Europe to the Crusader states. Bandits and Muslim soldiers were a constant threat to pilgrims, so the Templars built fortifications along the route to the Holy Land for security. They made full use of this network, transporting pilgrims and their belongings to the Holy Land, then bringing back goods from the Middle East to sell in Europe. Many regard the Templars as the first bankers, as they allowed travelers to deposit money and goods in Europe and withdraw them upon arrival in the Holy Land.

For almost two centuries, the Christians struggled to hold on to territory in the Holy Land and keep the Muslims at bay. While the Templars fought valiantly most of the time, Christian forces did not have enough armies and support from Western Europe to overcome massive numbers of Muslim warriors. Muslim factions often put aside their differences to attack the infidels invading their lands, while feudalistic Christian factions had problems maintaining cohesion, fighting among themselves on numerous occasions. Both sides showed little mercy to the other, slaughtering the entire population of seized cities and killing prisoners of war.

Twilight of the Templars

When Acre, the last Christian stronghold in Palestine, fell to the Muslims in 1291, fortunes changed for the Templars. Some blamed the Templars for the loss of the Holy Land. Others suggested merging the Templars with another holy order of knights, the Hospitallers. The last Grand Master of the Templars, Jacques de Molay, traveled to France to attempt to organize another crusade.

King Philip IV of France took advantage of this situation by hatching a plot to bring down the Templars so he could seize their wealth for himself. The king had incurred heavy debts in his war with England and owed the Templars a significant sum. After his wife died, Philip applied to join the Templars but was denied entry, only adding to his animosity toward them. During riots in Paris over his monetary policies in June 1306, Philip took refuge in a Templar stronghold for three days, where he must have noticed their conspicuous wealth and power.

The greed of King Philip knew no bounds. He engaged in currency manipulation, increased taxation, and bullied or arrested anyone who stood in his way. In 1306, the king levied heavy taxes on the Jews, then later arrested and exiled them in order to seize their assets and cancel his debt. The Templars became his next target.

Technically, the Templars still answered only to the pope, so Philip used his power and influence to install a puppet to the papal throne, Pope Clement V, then moved that throne from Rome to Avignon, France. After fabricating elaborate charges of heresy, Philip issued secret orders throughout France to arrest all Templars and seize their assets on the morning of Friday, October 13, 1307.

The surprise raids caught the Templars off guard; very few escaped the French authorities. Philip wanted the Templars interrogated immediately. At the time, interrogation meant severe and brutal torture until the subject confessed. Many Templars simply confessed to avoid the horrible ordeal of torture. Others died as a result of torture. Jacques de Molay confessed but withdrew his confession during a public spectacle at Notre Dame on March 18, 1314. Those who revoked their confessions were executed, and the authorities burned de Molay at the stake that evening. As he died, he cursed both pope and king.

Heads and Idols

The 127 articles of accusation, drawn up in 1309, charged the Templars with committing many common heretical acts, such as denying Christ, defiling the cross, profaning the sacrament, and engaging in sodomy. Strangely, many of the accusations concerned the nature and worship of idols or heads:

Article X

> That in all provinces these brothers had idols in the form of heads, some of which had three faces, some one, and some had a human skull;

That they worshiped those idols or that idol, and in particular in their general chapters and gatherings;

That they worshiped it or them;

That they worshiped it or them as God;

That they worshiped it or them as Saviour;

That some of them did;

That the majority of them did;

That they said that the head could save them;

That it made them rich;

That it gave them all their riches.

That it made the soil bring forth seeds;

That it made the trees flower.

That they encircled or touched some head with cords which they then tied around their shirt and bodies;

That at reception the small cords, or others of the same length, were handed to each brother;

That this was done in veneration of the idol;

That they were told to tie said cords around them as said previously and to wear them at all times;

That this was also done at night.[1]

Descriptions of this head or heads gleaned from confessions vary considerably because the heads probably never existed; extensive searches of Templar preceptories found no idols or heads. Tortured templars simply described whatever their inquisitors wanted to hear: they venerated a bearded head or three heads made out of wood, or gold, or silver; it had no legs or four legs; it took the shape of a demon or a cat. Unfortunately, these erratic confessions, completely unreliable, have often served as the basis of historical fanta-

1. Malcolm Barber and Keith Bate, *The Templars* (Manchester University Press, 2002), 275–276.

sies and conspiracy theories regarding the Templars. We now know that torture is a very unreliable method of gathering information. Every person has a pain threshold, and once that threshold is crossed, they will tell their tormentor anything they want to hear—that the moon is made of cheese, that they practice witchcraft in service of Satan, or that they worship an idol named Baphomet.

The name "Baphomet" does not appear in King Philip's arrest warrants, in the articles of accusation, or in any of the papal bulls issued by Pope Clement V. So how did the name Baphomet become associated with these monstrous heads?

The answer comes from the confessions of tortured templars in the southern regions of France who called the idol "Baphomet." In the Occitan tongue spoken in southern France and northern Spain, "Baphomet" referred to "Mahomet" or Mohammed. The fact that Islam prohibits both the worship of idols and images of Mohammed demonstrates that the church inquisitors knew nothing about the Muslim faith and sought only to defame the Templars by suggesting they had converted to Islam during their many years in the Holy Land.[2] The name Baphomet endured, and the connection to Mahomet/Mohammed was soon lost to history.

This historical origin of the name Baphomet is a recent discovery. Yet for centuries prior, people attempted to deduce the meaning of the name. Strangely enough, many interpretations connected the name with wisdom, which, as we will see in part three, was correct.

Nothing favorable came out of the Templars' trial. King Philip found no significant Templar treasure in Paris or anywhere else in France. The Templar fleet had sailed out of their main naval base in La Rochelle the day before the arrests and disappeared. Finally,

---

2. Peter Partner, *The Knights Templar and Their Myth* (Destiny, 1990), 78.

the curse uttered by de Molay as he burned at the stake came to pass—both pope and king died within a year of his execution.

The Masonic Revolution

Almost four hundred years later, the Freemasons, the mystical fraternal order that emerged at the beginning of the eighteenth century, claimed (among other things) that they were descendants of the Knights Templar, whom they characterized as noble men wrongly accused and convicted by church and state. The establishment of the Scottish Rite degrees in 1801 (itself based on the concept of a Masonic knighthood with Templar trimmings) cemented the connection between the two groups. The popularity of Masonry also fostered independent Neo-Templar lodges in Europe (particularly in Germany) by men nostalgic for the nobility and chivalry of knighthood and inspired by the idea that the Templars had possessed an ancient wisdom gleaned from their adventures in the Holy Land.

However, the aristocracy and the Catholic Church considered the Masons' secretive meetings and promotion of equality and religious tolerance subversive. In 1738, the church prohibited Catholics from seeking membership, issuing the first of many proclamations by the Vatican against Freemasonry. The connection between the Masons and the Templars, with the former glorifying the latter, also did not sit well with the Catholic Church.

One of the most successful anti-Masons who used the supposed guilt of the Templars to cast a shadow on the Masons was Jesuit priest and conspiracy theorist Augustin Barruel, author of *Memoirs Illustrating the History of Jacobinism* (1798), in which he accused the Masons of orchestrating the French Revolution to bring down the king and the church.

The French Revolution had devastated the Catholic Church in France. The many privileges it possessed as the official religion of

France were lost during the brutal dechristianization imposed by the left-wing Jacobins during the French Revolution. The powerful First Estate was decimated, as a large number of clergy were killed or exiled. Formerly the single largest landowner in France, the church saw its property seized and sold off by the state. Although France remained a predominately Catholic country throughout the nineteenth century, the Catholic Church never regained the power and wealth that it possessed before the Revolution.

Barruel blamed this catastrophe on a vast anti-Christian conspiracy stretching back to the establishment of Manichaeism, a "conspiracy" perpetuated by the Gnostics, the Cathars, the Templars, and the Illuminati that had been carried out by the Masons. He warped Jacques de Molay's curse on King Philip IV and Pope Clement V into an oath of vengeance to destroy the monarchy and the Catholic Church, supposedly fulfilled by the Masons during the French Revolution:

> Nor is it necessary in this place to examine whether *Molay* and his Order were innocent or criminal, whether they were the real progenitors of the Free-masons or not; what is incontestable is sufficient; it is enough that the Masons recognize them for their ancestors; then the oath of avenging them and every allegory recalling that oath decidedly points out an association, continually threatening and conspiring against Religion and its Pontiffs, against Empires and their Governors.[3]

Barruel's *Memoirs* was one of the first popular works to promote the idea of an active Masonic conspiracy against church and state. It linked the Templars to the Masons and used the curse of

3. Augustin Barruel, *Memoirs Illustrating the History of Jacobinism* (American Council on Economics and Society, 1995), 340–41.

de Molay to demonize both groups. The book became a bestseller in France; an English translation of the first half of the work came out that same year and was soon translated into other languages.

The Myth of Baphomet Revealed

The first significant essay regarding Baphomet and the Templars is commonly known as "The Mysteries of Baphomet Revealed," published in 1818 by Austrian orientalist Joseph von Hammer-Purgstall. Unfortunately, the essay is a work of fiction penned for the purpose of discrediting Freemasonry.

Hammer-Purgstall's true motives are revealed in the full title of the essay: "The Mysteries of Baphomet Revealed, by which the Knights Templars, like the Gnostics and Ophites, are convicted of apostasy, of idolatry and of moral impurity, by their own monuments." Hammer-Purgstall's goal was to use this Templar connection against the Masons. His essay identified carvings and engravings of Baphomet supposedly found on thirteenth-century Templar artifacts he claimed proved that the Templars were guilty of idolatry and showed that Freemasonry had its roots in a heretical and criminal order. He also claimed that the Templars were the successors to the heretical Gnostics and that Baphomet was a Gnostic idol. He proposed that the name Baphomet meant "Baptism of Wisdom," and that the wisdom referred to was *Sophia* (Greek: "wisdom"), a major theme in Gnosticism. Finally, some of the images in his essay depicted orgies that included children and animals, resurrecting the idea that the Templars' secret rites included sexual perversion.

Many historians consider Hammer-Purgstall's essay spurious, and no one has been able to locate the sources of the images of the Templar artifacts featured in his essay. Because these images cannot be located and verified, there is no actual proof that the images are connected to the Templars in any way. There is no obvious symbolism or writing in the images that specifically connects them to the Templars. The only connection appears to be Hammer-Purgstall himself. Nonetheless, the spurious work's academic tone lent it an air of authority that led to frequent citations and wider distribution, perpetuating the farce. Hammer-Purgstall's essay renewed interest in the connection of Baphomet with the Templars and provided a subtle link between Baphomet and the Masons.

The Taxil Hoax

The Baphomet-Masonic conspiracy came to a head in France at the end of the nineteenth century. Gabriel Jogand-Pagès (1854–1907), who went by the pen name Leo Taxil, was originally known as the author and publisher of a number of sacrilegious and lurid anti-clerical books in the early 1880s. These included *The Secret Love Affairs of Pius IX* (1881) and *The Mistresses of the Pope* (1884), works that disparaged the papacy with scandalous, semi-pornographic stories of fictional love affairs; the former work landed Taxil in the courts, where he was successfully prosecuted for libel and heavily fined. In 1881, Taxil joined the local Masonic lodge thinking he'd find more converts for his anti-clerical cause, but instead he was expelled for publishing pornography. Things were not looking up for Taxil when his archenemy, Pope Leo XIII, unknowingly presented him with an opportunity to get back at both the church and the Masons.

As mentioned earlier, historical events in the nineteenth century had not been favorable to the Catholic Church. In 1870, the First Vatican Council issued the document *Pastor aeternus*, which declared and defined the infallibility of the pope. A year later, people living in the Papal States on the Italian peninsula revolted, seized power, and eventually united to form the Kingdom of Italy, and the infallible pope had no kingdom outside of Rome. The church had lost all of its land and most of its wealth, and revolutions had brought new governments to power that no longer needed nor sought the approval of the Vatican.

When Leo XIII ascended the papal throne in 1878, he inherited a much different church than his predecessors. The decline of the Catholic Church could not have happened under the rule of infallible popes; some evil external force opposed to the church must be to blame. Some Catholic authors, reciting Barruel's conspiracy, implicated Freemasons as the instigators of revolution and the advocates of equality, individual liberty, and freedom of religion—radical ideas that threatened the power of the church. Having found his scapegoat, Leo XIII issued the encyclical *Humanum Genus* in 1884, which cast Freemasonry as a great evil threatening the Catholic Church, and he advised Catholics around the world to be on the lookout for evidence of this Masonic threat. Leo Taxil gave it to them.

Taxil renounced his anti-clerical ways and confessed his sins to a Catholic priest. In 1886, Taxil started publishing exposés that connected the Masons with Lucifer, revealing the existence of Palladian Masonry, a secret order within the secretive order that sought to destroy the Catholic Church. Palladian Masonry admitted women, who were sworn in service to Lucifer and even consorted with demons. As Taxil's hoax evolved, his details became more lurid and scandalous.

An advertisement for Taxil's *The Mysteries of Freemasonry Unveiled*

Taxil used Éliphas Lévi's image of Baphomet as the face of his Masonic Lucifer. In 1887, posters promoting Taxil's newest work, *The Mysteries of Freemasonry Unveiled,* featured a perversion of Lévi's image redrawn with Masonic and Satanic symbolism. The image on the cover of the book and other illustrations within show the Masons worshiping idols based on Lévi's Baphomet. In later works, the Palladium locates and acquires the original Baphomet idol worshiped by the Templars and manufactures Baphomet idols and other diabolical equipment for Palladian lodges at secret factories in the rock of Gibraltar. It gets pretty wacky!

Taxil's hoax was very successful. Within a couple of years he got an audience with Pope Leo XIII, who was thrilled to have evidence of the evil Masonic plot against the church. Other authors in the Catholic press joined the anti-Masonic crusade, citing Taxil's revelations as truth and offering their own revelations and interpretations. But after a decade, the hoax started to fall apart, and Taxil decided it was time for people to know the truth. He organized a press conference in Paris, where he calmly and jovially explained that the church had been thoroughly hoaxed. He named his collaborators and their roles, all the while reveling in their shock and dismay. When he finished, there was such an uproar from the crowd that the police had to escort Taxil from the building.

The trial of the Templars linked the sins of the Order with the idolatry of Baphomet. When the Masons claimed to be descendants of the Templars, their detractors used that connection to demonize them and link them with the supposedly Satanic Baphomet. Then a con man with a grudge against the Catholic

Church and the Freemasons made a Luciferian Baphomet the face of a worldwide anti-Masonic hoax. Yet beyond the minds of conspiracy theorists and gullible Christians, there is absolutely no connection between Freemasonry and Baphomet or Satan.

However, the works of these conspirators still managed to influence people's perceptions of Baphomet. Both Éliphas Lévi and Aleister Crowley used Hammer-Purgstall's essay as source material when they wrote about Baphomet. Modern Fundamentalist Christians have mined books written during the Taxil Hoax for proof of Satanism in Masonry and found links to Baphomet. Ironic, considering that the creator of the occult icon of Baphomet didn't believe in Satan at all, as you'll see in the next chapter.

SOLVE
COAGULA
ELIPHAS
LEVI DEL.

Chapter 2

The Creation of Baphomet

In nineteenth-century France, the name Baphomet was maligned by conspiracy theorists, con men, and clergy in their efforts to demonize the Freemasons. France was also the birthplace of the esoteric Baphomet, created in 1856 by French occultist Éliphas Lévi. His image of Baphomet established the standard iconography for the deity, and the characteristics of his image significantly influenced all subsequent conceptions of Baphomet. In order to understand the symbolism and meaning of Lévi's Baphomet, you need to know a little about the life of Their creator.

Enter Éliphas Lévi

Alphonse Louis Constant was born at the family home in Paris on February 8, 1810. His poor Catholic parents baptized him three days later at Saint Sulpice Church, marking the beginning of Constant's contentious personal relationship with the Catholic Church that dominated the first part of his life. Constant was encouraged to pursue the priesthood after he took his First Communion, so at age fifteen, he entered the junior seminary at Saint Nicholas du Chardonnet, where he learned Hebrew, Latin, and Greek; at eighteen, he could read scriptures in the original Hebrew. But shortly after he received his ordination as a deacon in 1835, Constant developed a platonic affection for one of his students, a girl named Adele Allenbach. Questioning his vows on the eve of attaining the priesthood, the conflicted twenty-six-year-old Constant left the seminary. He rejoined the church a few years later, but friction with church officials due to his political activism led to a series of disappointing and discouraging experiences; Constant formally renounced his holy orders and finally severed his ties with the Catholic Church in 1842.

In 1837, he had met socialist and feminist activist Flora Tristan at an artists' workshop, and the two became good friends. Tristan and another friend, Alphonse Esquiros, encouraged Constant to join them in political activism, and he started to develop his own ideas about Christian socialism and feminism. He wrote a number of subversive political works, three of which earned him time in prison: eleven months for "The Bible of Liberty" (1841), a radical Christian socialist tract; six months for "The Voice of Hunger" (1847), a seditious pamphlet that criticized social inequality in France; and a brief imprisonment for "Caligula" (1855), a poem that compared Napoleon III to the tyrannical Roman emperor.

In 1848, the government of France underwent many radical changes. King Louis-Philippe abdicated on February 24, and the declaration of the Second Republic soon followed. Elections in April produced a Constituent Assembly to rule France, but conflicts with French radicals led to fighting in the streets of Paris between radicals and government troops on June 23; the soldiers defeated the rebels a few days later in what became known as the June Days uprising. In December, the Constituent Assembly elected Louis Napoleon Bonaparte to serve as president, the politician who became Napoleon III and established the Second Empire four years later.

Constant and his socialist compatriots were actively involved in these political events, writing articles for short-lived journals, forming political clubs, and even demonstrating in the streets. Constant published his last socialist work, *The Testament of Liberty*, in July 1848. He made an unsuccessful attempt to represent the people in the Constituent Assembly, and when Esquiros was elected in May 1849, the friendship between them soured. Constant started to drift away from politics.

Constant indulged his latent interest in mysticism and started studying Qabala and other occult sciences, encouraged by a brief friendship with Polish émigré Josef Hoëné-Wronski. Around this time, Constant started using the pseudonym Éliphas Lévi, a Hebraicized translation of "Alphonse Louis." Under his new pseudonym, he published *Doctrine of High Magic* in 1854 and *Ritual of High Magic* in 1855; a single volume edition, *Doctrine and Ritual of High Magic*, came out in 1856. The book became Lévi's magnum opus, introducing magic and occultism to a mainstream audience. It was one of the first books to explore and popularize the connection between the twenty-two letters of the Hebrew alphabet and the twenty-two tarot trumps, a connection so significant to Lévi that he divided both the "Doctrine" and "Ritual" sections of his book into twenty-two chapters. His book also contained his most popular and misunderstood artistic work, the image of Baphomet, which can be found in this book on page 26.

Lévi published two more popular books on occultism, *The History of Magic* in 1860 and *The Key of the Great Mysteries* in 1861. Lévi's fame as a master of the occult sciences soon spread across the channel to England, prompting two visits to London, one in 1854 and another in 1861. Lévi was also in contact with the esoteric

English masons of the *Societas Rosicruciana in Anglia* (Rosicrucian Society of England) through one of its members, English occult scholar and fringe Mason Kenneth MacKenzie, who visited Lévi in Paris at the end of 1861. After Lévi's death, members of the Societas Rosicruciana formed the Hermetic Order of the Golden Dawn, whose philosophy and magic were influenced by Lévi's works and whose membership included Arthur Edward Waite and Aleister Crowley, occultists who translated Lévi's major works into English.

Lévi attracted students and disciples of the occult who were seeking instruction, and he made a meager living giving lessons that sustained him for the rest of his life. He continued to write books on occult subjects, though none proved to be as popular as his first three works. Lévi died on May 31, 1875. At his funeral, his friends and students gathered at his graveside to pay their respects, including Adele Allenbach, now bent with age.

The Astral Light

Lévi's image of Baphomet is a complex symbol that incorporates many different but related interpretations based on his occult philosophy. First and foremost, however, Baphomet is a representation of one of the most important concepts presented in *Doctrine and Ritual*: the astral light.

In the introduction to *Doctrine and Ritual*, Lévi proclaims the existence of a powerful magical force. He writes:

> There exists in Nature a force which is immeasurably more powerful than steam, and a single man, who is able to adapt and direct it, might change thereby the face of the whole world. This force was known to the ancients; it consists in a Universal Agent having equilibrium for its supreme law, while its direction is concerned

> immediately with the Great Arcanum of Transcendental Magic.... This agent, which barely manifests under the uncertain methods of Mesmer's followers, is precisely that which the adepts of the Middle Ages denominated the First Matter of the Great Work. The Gnostics represented it as the fiery body of the Holy Spirit; it was the object of adoration in the Secret Rites of the Sabbath and the Temple, under the hieroglyphic figure of Baphomet or the Androgyne of Mendes.[4]

Lévi describes the astral light as an invisible spiritual substance: "It is the vital element which manifests itself by the phenomena of heat, light, electricity, and magnetism, which magnetizes all terrestrial globes, and all living beings."[5] As the astral light exists everywhere within the universe, it also connects all things within the universe, and thus it serves as the basis for all occult operations. All actions, emotions, and thoughts leave impressions in the astral light, so it also serves as a spiritual record of all things that happen in the universe. According to Lévi, the astral light is analogous with the fifth element of spirit.

The belief in an invisible spiritual force was neither new nor unique to occultism. The same concept can be found in ancient shamanism as well as many other religions. Lévi himself was influenced by the works of Franz Mesmer and his ideas about animal magnetism as well as scientific discoveries in the nineteenth century regarding the natural forces of electricity. While Lévi was not the first to conceive of the astral light, his works popularized the

---

4. Éliphas Lévi, *Transcendental Magic: Its Doctrine and Ritual,* trans. A. E. Waite (Samuel Weiser, 1999; originally published 1896), 12.
5. Éliphas Lévi, *The Key of the Mysteries,* trans. Aleister Crowley (Samuel Weiser, 2002; originally published 1861 as *La Clef des Grands Mystères Suivant Hénoch, Abraham, Hermès Trismégiste et Salomon* by Germer-Baillière), 147.

concept within Western esotericism. Influential esoteric groups that emerged during the last part of the nineteenth century, like the Theosophical Society and The Hermetic Order of the Golden Dawn, incorporated Lévi's concept of the astral light into their own occult systems. The Golden Dawn and its legacy influenced other notable occultists, including Aleister Crowley and Peter Carroll.

Lévi used the astral light to explain unusual phenomena such as somnambulism, dreams, hauntings, spiritism, madness, and lycanthropy. More importantly, he established the astral light as the medium by which all operations of traditional esoteric disciplines such as astrology, alchemy, necromancy, sorcery, and divination are accomplished. Astral light was one of the concepts Lévi used to unite these different esoteric disciplines under the newly minted term of occultism.

Lévi taught that if we use our faculties of intelligence, will, and imagination to project our desires into the astral light with enough force and clarity, we can cause changes to manifest in the physical world—we can perform magic. However, some preparation is necessary, for like other natural forces, the astral light is a neutral force that can be used for good or evil. In *Doctrine and Ritual*, Lévi wrote:

> The Astral Light, depicted in ancient symbols by the serpent devouring its tail, represents alternately malice and prudence, time and eternity, tempter and Redeemer; for this light, being the vehicle of life, is an auxiliary alike of good and evil, and may be taken not only for the fiery form of Satan but for the body of the Holy Ghost.[6]

---

6. Lévi, *Transcendental Magic*, 85.

Lévi often used the serpent as a symbol for the astral light, likening the snake's undulating movement to the flow of the astral currents. The serpent devouring its tail, or ouroboros serpent, is a symbol of the eternal cycle of life, death, and rebirth.

Lévi thought that living beings, as part of the astral light, are subject to the ebb and flow of its invisible currents, as well as to the astral projections and manipulations of others around us. Furthermore, he believed that elementals and spirits lived within the astral light and that they could influence or interfere with people's lives in the material world. Lévi recommended that those seeking to work with the astral light foster equilibrium and harmony within themselves by developing inner tranquility, emotional control, and an indomitable will.

A Magical Icon

Lévi's Baphomet image illustrates the idealized nature of the astral light. Baphomet has the body of an androgyne, inspired in part by the winged androgyne that dominates the Devil trump of the Marseilles tarot deck and the androgyne from an image in a sixteenth-century alchemical text by German physician and philosopher Heinrich Khunrath.[7] In alchemy, the androgyne signifies a harmonious combination and balance of masculine and feminine energies, often represented by the sun and the moon. Like Khunrath's Androgyne, Baphomet has a masculine arm inscribed with *solve* and a feminine arm inscribed with *coagula*; the formula *solve et coagula* ("dissolve and coagulate") describes the process of alchemy in its most simplistic terms.

One of Baphomet's arms points upward and the other down, a gesture that indicates the great axiom of Hermeticism that connects

7. Heinrich Khunrath, *Amphitheatrum sapientiae aeternae*, 1595, figure 4. This image is described in the next section.

the macrocosm with the microcosm: "as above, so below." Each hand makes what Lévi calls the "sign of esotericism"[8] and the "sign of occultism."[9] In the Catholic Church, this gesture is well known as the sign of benediction used by popes in blessings; the meaning and origin of Lévi's terminology is unknown.

Baphomet is pointing toward two crescent moons, one light and the other dark, which Lévi identifies with Chesed and Geburah, two spheres of the Tree of Life, the central glyph of the Qabala. These spheres represent the two pillars of Mercy and Severity, and placing Baphomet between them identifies the figure with the harmonizing middle pillar of Balance.

The pentagram with a single point upright on Baphomet's forehead represents the "empire of will over the Astral Light, which is the physical soul of the four elements."[10] When projected upon the human body with the head in the ascendant point, the pentagram signifies the domination of the mind or spirit over the four elements of matter. To Lévi, the pentagram had the power to project or contain energy, and it could also be used to compel evil spirits or protect one from their influence.

Regarding the pentagram and the torch, Lévi states: "On its forehead, between the horns and beneath the torch, is the sign of the Microcosm, or the Pentagram with one point in the ascendant, a symbol of human intelligence, which, placed thus below the torch, makes the flame of the latter an image of divine revelation."[11] Here Lévi implies that the torch above the microcosmic pentagram is a symbol of the macrocosm, indicating that the astral light also serves

---

8. Lévi, *Transcendental Magic*, xiv.
9. Lévi, *Transcendental Magic*, 309.
10. Lévi, *Transcendental Magic*, 67.
11. Lévi, *Transcendental Magic*, xiv–xv.

as our connection to the Divine. He also tells us: "The torch of intelligence burning between the horns is the magical light of universal equilibrium; it is also the type of the soul exalted above matter, even while cleaving to matter, as the flame cleaves to the torch."[12] The flame, which is associated with divine revelation, universal equilibrium, and the soul, represents the highest and most spiritual expression of the astral light. The horns and torch suggest the shape of the Hebrew letter Shin, a symbol of fire, as indicated in *The Key of the Mysteries*:

> The thirty-first [path of the Qabala] refers to [the Hebrew letter Shin], which represents the magic lamp, or the light between the horns of Baphomet. It is the qabalistic sign of the OD, or astral light, with its two poles, and its balanced centre.[13]

A veil covers the lower part of Baphomet's body, concealing the genitals, which are symbolized by the caduceus, the wand of Mercury, a symbol of eternal life and the mysteries of universal generation. The caduceus can also be interpreted to signify the conjunction of male and female sex organs, with the snakes forming the vagina and womb and the staff the penetrating phallus. The intertwined snakes are black and white, suggesting the union of polarized forces.

To stress that the astral light is part of all living things, Lévi has given Baphomet characteristics of different forms of terrestrial life: a scaled belly signifying fish and reptiles; feathers (above the belly) and wings signifying birds; the goat's head and hooves signifying mammals; and breasts, torso, and arms signifying humans. The Baphomet image also contains symbolism that connects it with the

12. Lévi, *Transcendental Magic*, 309.
13. Lévi, *The Key of the Mysteries*, 157.

four elements: the fish scales indicate Water; the feathers, Air; the cube, Earth; and the torch, Fire. The cube Baphomet sits on is a symbol of matter, signifying the intimate connection that the astral light has with the material world, just as Spirit is connected to the other elements.

Overall, the image of Baphomet conveys the significance of magical equilibrium in operations of the astral light. Lévi placed Baphomet at the center point between symbols of polar forces or concepts such as light and dark, mercy and justice, etc. Likewise, the figure of Baphomet itself manifests as the union of opposites: male and female, *solve et coagula*, human intelligence and divine revelation, animal instincts and human reason, body and soul. Baphomet is not just an image of the astral light but a completely equilibrated, harmonious expression of that universal agent.

Alchemy and Azoth

Alchemy is one of the pillars of Lévi's system of occultism. Lévi was familiar with the works of many of the great alchemists and mentions them frequently in *Doctrine and Ritual*, including Nicolas Flamel, Basil Valentinus, Raymond Lully, Heinrich Khunrath and, above all, Paracelsus. While he did not have the financial means to establish his own alchemical laboratory, Lévi did practice alchemy with people he met through his books, affluent friends with the proper equipment and facilities. His fascination with alchemy is reflected in the Baphomet image; in *Doctrine and Ritual*, Lévi cites two alchemical images that influenced his construction of Baphomet.

The first influence is the Androgyne of Khunrath, briefly mentioned above. This image was featured in Khunrath's *Amphitheatrum sapientiae aeternae* (*Amphitheater of Eternal Wisdom*), a book heralded by Lévi as "a true manual of Transcendental Magic and

Hermetic Philosophy" that "contains all mysteries of the highest initiation."[14] Khunrath's work combined Christianity with alchemy and magic, a synthesis that Lévi must have found very appealing.

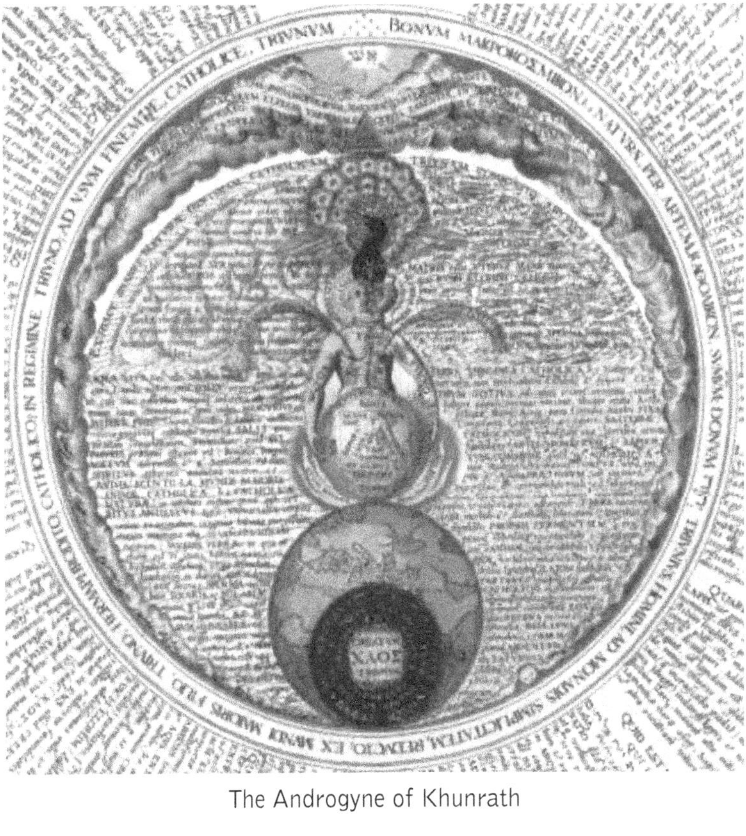

The Androgyne of Khunrath

Khunrath's androgyne emerges from a sphere of the first matter *(materia prima)* set atop a terrestrial globe. The sphere is heated by fire. The androgyne is male on the left side and female on the

14. Lévi, *The History of Magic*, trans. A. E. Waite (Samuel Weiser, 2001; originally published 1859 by Rider & Co), 266.

right side and has two heads, one for each gender. The chest of the androgyne bears the alchemical symbol of sulfur on the right breast, the salt symbol on the left breast, and the symbol of mercury on the navel. The male head is crowned with the sun and the female head crowned with the moon. Sitting on their heads is a raven labeled "AZOTH," with the O extended into the astrological sigil of Mercury. The raven has two extra sets of wings: a pair of multicolored eagle wings and a fan of peacock feathers. Lévi found the arms of the androgyne particularly significant: the masculine arm is inscribed with *solve* and the feminine arm with *coagula*.

Nuysement's Androgyne

Another alchemical source that influenced Baphomet comes from a seventeenth-century alchemical treatise by French alchemist and poet Clovis Hesteau, sieur de Nuysement. Lévi describes the image in *Doctrine and Ritual*:

> The spirit of the earth is represented standing on a cube over which tongues of flame are passing; the phallus is replaced by a caduceus; the sun and moon figure on the right and left breast; the figure is bearded, crowned, and holds a sceptre in his hand. This is the AZOTH of the sages on its pedestal of Salt and Sulphur. The symbolic head of the goat of Mendes is occasionally given to this figure, and it is then the Baphomet of the Templars and the Word of the Gnostics—bizarre images which became scarecrows for the vulgar after affording food for reflection to sages—innocent hieroglyphs of thought and faith which have been a pretext for the rage of persecutions.[15]

Here Lévi hints that Baphomet also signifies azoth, suggesting an alchemical interpretation of the Baphomet image. If you reexamine the image of Baphomet through the lens of alchemy, it becomes a symbol of azoth like Khunrath's and Nuysement's androgynes.

The original purpose of alchemy was the transformation and purification of materials like plants and metals; in modern times, the alchemical process is more often used as an allegory for the spiritual transformation and purification of the human psyche. This process of transformation and purification is known as the Great Work. One of the primary goals of alchemy is to create the philosopher's stone, a substance that was reported to purify all metals and cure all illnesses. In the works of the famed sixteenth-century Swiss alchemist Paracelsus, this stone was often referred to as azoth.

15. Lévi, *Transcendental Magic*, 168.

The word "azoth" is derived from the Arabic word for the metal mercury, *al-za'buq*. Azoth is sometimes referred to as philosophical mercury, for as the alchemical element of mercury is often conceived as the fluidic mediator between the alchemical elements of earthy salt and fiery sulfur, azoth serves as the mediator between salt, sulfur, and mercury, serving the same function as mercury but on a more spiritual level. In terms of the five elements, Lévi attributed azoth to spirit, sulfur to fire, salt to earth, and mercury to air and water. He also identified azoth with the astral light.

The Alchemical Baphomet

Lévi warns us that "all masters in alchemy who have written concerning the Great Work have employed symbolical and figurative expressions, and have been right in so doing, not only to deter the profane from operations which would be dangerous for them, but to make themselves intelligible to adepts by revealing the entire world of analogies. . . ."[16] One of the primary difficulties in deciphering alchemical symbolism is that the interpretations of these symbolic and figurative expressions are often inconsistent among works authored by different alchemists. For example, take the number of steps or stages required to perform the operation to achieve the Great Work. Some alchemy texts give only two, *solve et coagula*; others offer three or four stages based on the colors associated with each stage, the *nigredo* (blackening), *albedo* (whitening), *citrinitas* (yellowing, sometimes considered part of the *albedo*), and *rubedo* (reddening); another work might present seven steps that correspond with the seven classical planets, or twelve steps that correspond with the signs of the zodiac. The goal is the same, but

16. Lévi, *Transcendental Magic*, 282.

the path to that goal can be described in many ways. The point is that a large part of deciphering the alchemical symbolism of Baphomet is determining what these symbols and concepts meant specifically to Éliphas Lévi.

Lévi states that azoth is composed of an ideal relationship between the alchemical elements:

> The first matter of the Great Work... is Sulphur, Mercury and Salt, which, volatized and fixed alternately, compose the AZOTH of the sages. Sulphur corresponds to the elementary form of fire, Mercury to air and water, Salt to earth.[17]

These elements also represent alchemical principles: "Alchemically, salt is the principle of solidity, mercury of fluidity, sulfur of volatility, and azoth is the universal solvent that permits their separation and recombination."[18] The figure of Baphomet symbolizes the combination of the three alchemical elements in Azoth. Lévi knew that the cube that Baphomet sits on is a common alchemical symbol for salt: "... their Salt is represented under the form of a cubical stone, as we can observe in the TWELVE KEYS of Basil Valentine, or in the allegories of Trevisan."[19] He also knew that the caduceus is a symbol associated with mercury, as is the androgynous human body: "Mercury is the winged and bearded Hermaphrodite, throned upon a cube and crowned with flames."[20]

The goat or goat head is not a common alchemical symbol, but Lévi defines it in alchemical terms twice in *Doctrine and Ritual*:

---

17. Lévi, *Transcendental Magic*, 281–82.
18. Éliphas Lévi, *The Doctrine and Ritual of High Magic: A New Translation*, trans. Mark Anthony Mikituk. (TarcherPerigee, 2017), 63 fn.
19. Lévi, *Transcendental Magic*, 164.
20. Lévi, *Transcendental Magic*, 282.

> The bull, the dog, and the goat are the three symbolical animals of Hermetic Magic, resuming all the traditions of Egypt and India. The bull represents the Earth or Salt of the Philosophers; the dog is Hermanubis, the Mercury of the sages—otherwise, fluid, air and water; the goat represents fire and is at the same time the symbol of generation.[21]

If the bull represents salt and the dog is mercury, it follows that the goat represents fiery sulfur. The goat/sulfur attribution is also mentioned later in the book:

> To express hieroglyphically this law of prudence, the sages ascribed to their Mercury, personified in Egypt as Hermanubis, a dog's head, and to their Sulphur, represented by the Baphomet of the Temple or Prince of the Sabbath, that goat's head which brought such odium upon the occult associations of the middle ages.[22]

Salt (cube), mercury (caduceus/androgyne), and sulfur (goat head) together compose azoth (Baphomet). The wings signify the combination is volatile and the figure sitting on a cube signifies the combination is fixed, so the three alchemical elements have been "volatized and fixed alternately" as mentioned above. The presence of azoth is indicated by the "torch of intelligence … the magical light of universal equilibrium"[23] which, like Khunrath's azoth-labeled crow, is placed above the head.

---

21. Lévi, *Transcendental Magic,* 308. This quote is taken from chapter 15 of *Ritual;* it appears a few paragraphs before Lévi describes his Baphomet image.
22. Lévi, *Transcendental Magic,* 359.
23. Lévi, *Transcendental Magic,* 309.

The arms inscribed with *solve* and *coagula* have a special significance:

> The Great Magical Agent, by us termed the Astral Light, by others the soul of the earth, and designated by old alchemists under the names of AZOTH and MAGNESIA, this occult, unique and indubitable force, is the key of all empire, the secret of all power. ... To know how to make use of this Agent is to be the trustee of God's own power; all real, effective Magic, all occult force is there, and its demonstration is the sole end of all genuine books of science. To have control over the Great Magical Agent there are two operations necessary–to concentrate and project, or, in other words, to fix and to move.[24]

In alchemy, these two operations are labeled *solve* and *coagula*, and it is through this simple formula that one may create the proper combination of the alchemical elements and form azoth. Both Khunrath and Lévi inscribed the formula on their androgyne's arms to indicate that this can be achieved through human labor, either physical or metaphysical.

Socialist Androgynes

So far we've only talked about alchemical androgynes, symbols of the combination and integration of male and female principles like the sun and the moon. However, Lévi first encountered the symbol of the androgyne not in alchemical or occult works but in the works of Romantic socialists published during the July Monarchy (1830–1848), back when he was still known as Alphonse Louis Constant.

24. Lévi, *Transcendental Magic*, 104.

The Romantic socialists of the early nineteenth century differed in significant ways from modern French socialists. Secularism is an integral part of modern French socialism, but the first proponents of socialism in the nineteenth century were Romantics, valuing emotion and imagination over Enlightenment-based reason and rationality, and thus their works often contain mystic, religious, and utopian themes. Many of the first socialists were also feminists, as the Napoleonic Code severely restricted women's rights; the Romantic socialists sought to promote equality among workers and genders. In the 1840s, Constant became one of their most vocal advocates.

Constant's first major encounter with the political androgyne came in 1839, when his friend Alphonse Esquiros took him to meet the Mapah, the alter-ego of eccentric socialist Simon Ganneau. The event had such an impact on Constant that he recounted it in *The History of Magic*:

> In an appalling garret, there was a bearded man of majestic demeanor who habitually wore over his clothes the tattered cloak of a woman, which made him look rather like a destitute dervish. He was surrounded by several men, bearded and ecstatic like himself, and by a woman with motionless features who seemed like an entranced somnambulist.
>
> His manner was abrupt but sympathetic, his eloquence emphatic, his eyes hallucinated; he spoke with emphasis, became animated, and raged and fumed till a white froth gathered on his lips.[25]

25. Lévi, *Histoire de la Magie* (Germer-Baillière, 1860), 520. Quote translated by Michael Osiris Snuffin.

Ganneau preached a new religion that fused Christian elements with socialist ideals and featured an androgyne, Evadam (Eve-Adam), as the herald of a new utopian age and Mary as the savior of humanity. Ganneau was the prophet and priest of this new religion as the androgynous Mapah (mater-pater).

Constant and Esquiros had come for entertainment but left inspired, "their imaginations overcome by his eloquence"; their encounters with Ganneau "gave birth" to Constant's *Bible of Liberty* and Esquiros's *Gospel of the People*, books that got the two friends thrown in prison.

Scholar Naomi J. Andrews recounts the significant impact that Ganneau had on Constant:

> Like Ganneau, Constant used Mary and Christ as archetypal figures of man and woman, and depicted them as united into a divine androgyne, heralding humanity's rebirth. Also like Ganneau, ... Constant identified the androgyne in feminine terms, linking it conceptually and strategically with the achievement of a feminized utopian society, ruled both by women and by feminine values.[26]

These ideas are prominent in two works Constant published after *The Bible of Liberty*. The first, written and published while in prison, was *The Assumption of Woman, or the Book of Love*, which included translations and commentaries on *The Songs of Songs* and the works of St. John of the Cross, St. Theresa, and Madame Guyon. There's a trend here: St. John of the Cross (1542–1591) was a Spanish Catholic priest known for his mystical theological poetry; Theresa of Avila (1515–1582) was a Spanish nun and author

26. Naomi J. Andrews, *Socialism's Muse: Gender in the Intellectual Landscape of French Romantic Socialism* (Lexington Books, 2006), 105.

of numerous works on Christian mysticism; and Madame Guyon (1648–1717) was a French mystic and author of numerous works on Christian mysticism. All three were influential advocates for Christian mysticism that were persecuted by the Catholic Church for their beliefs, an experience Lévi had become familiar with.

In *The Assumption of Woman*, Lévi proclaimed that Mary would be the redeemer who will usher humanity into the age of the Paraclete. When this new utopia rises, an androgyne forms:

> Such will be our new society. The two sexes will be but one, according to the word of Christ; the great androgyne will be created; humanity will be woman and man, love and thought, tenderness and force, grace and energy.[27]

The second book, *The Mother of God*, describes Constant's allegorical journey to a socialist utopia, where a female messiah takes him to meet the celestial mother who watches over humanity. Once again, his socialist utopia manifests as a symbolic androgyne:

> This is the palace of the husband and the wife; here lies the pure and celestial love; here exists no distinction between the ranks and sexes anymore; God alone is all in all.[28]

When Constant gazes at this new utopian society, he temporarily becomes absorbed into its androgyne:

---

27. Constant, *The Assumption of Woman*, 79; translated and quoted in Andrews, *Socialism's Muse*, 105.
28. Constant, *La Mère de Dieu*, 279. Translated and quoted in Julian Strube, "The Baphomet of Éliphas Lévi: Its Meaning and Historical Context" (*Correspondences* 4, 2016), 63.

> I felt that I lived in the same celestial air and in the same light as all other beings, and their lives became a part of my own. I would have suffered with them, and I rejoiced in their happiness.
>
> Their souls became a part of my soul and their thoughts were my own. I felt their hearts beat in my own breast.... We could no longer live without each other; we were like the members of a single body which have no separate lives of their own. I felt neither worry nor fear; all had found its harmony in the law of unity and surrounded me with the power of God himself.[29]

Curiously, Lévi's utopian androgyne has much in common with the astral light, which flows through and links all beings, records all thoughts and emotions, and bestows god-like powers when properly harmonized and equilibrated.

Constant used the symbol of the androgyne to represent the economic, sexual, and spiritual harmony that would manifest in a socialist utopia. The use of the androgyne as the basis for the Baphomet figure is thus an expression of Constant's utopian socialism that became integrated into Lévi's occult philosophy.

The Caprine Lineage

Throughout *Doctrine and Ritual*, Lévi associates Baphomet with three titles: the Goat of Mendes, the Baphomet of the Templars, and the Goat of the Sabbath. These titles establish a fictional lineage for the Baphomet image that provides more context to the goat symbolism therein.

---

29. Constant, *La Mère de Dieu*, 293. Translated and quoted in Thomas Williams, *Éliphas Lévi: Master of the Cabala, the Tarot and the Secret Doctrines* (Venture, 2003), 56.

Like many French occultists of the nineteenth century, Lévi linked elements of his occult philosophy to ancient cultures to give it a sense of historical and spiritual legitimacy. Our association of the goat with the ancient mysteries thus begins with the Goat of Mendes in Ancient Egypt. It is likely that Lévi learned about the Goat of Mendes from the *Histories* written by the ancient Greek historian Herodotus:

> I mentioned the fact that certain Egyptians (the Mendesians) will not sacrifice goats, either male or female. The reason is this: they believe Pan to be one of the eight gods who existed before the subsequent twelve, and painters and sculptors represent him just as the Greeks do, with the face and legs of a goat. Not that they think he is, in fact, like that—on the contrary they do not believe he differs in form from the rest of the gods. But that is how they paint him—why, I should prefer not to mention. The Mendesians hold all goats in veneration, especially male ones, whose keepers enjoy special honours. One of them is held in particular reverence, and when he dies the whole province goes into mourning. Mendes is the Egyptian name both for Pan and for a goat.[30]

The Goat of Mendes title associates Lévi's Baphomet with the veneration of goats in ancient Egypt and the god Pan of ancient Greece, establishing Baphomet's connection with antiquity. Lévi also appears to connect Baphomet with Pan in *Doctrine and Ritual*:

> Yes, in our profound conviction, the Grand Masters of the Order of the Templars worshiped the Baphomet and

30. Herodotus, *The Histories*, ed. John Marnicola, trans. Aubrey de Sélincourt (Penguin, 2003), 114–15.

> caused it to be worshiped by their initiates; yes, there existed in the past, and there may be still in the present, assemblies which are presided over by this figure, sitting on a throne and having a flaming torch between the horns. But the adorers of this sign do not consider, as do we, that it is the representation of the devil: on the contrary, for them it is that of the god Pan, the god of our modern schools of philosophy, the god of the Alexandrian theurgic school and of our own mystical Neoplatonists, the god of Lamartine and Victor Cousin, the god of Spinoza and Plato, the god of the primitive Gnostic schools; the Christ also of the dissident priesthood.[31]

Yet closer examination of this paragraph reveals that Lévi isn't really talking about the god Pan, but pantheism, the belief that the universe and the divine are a single entity. The fact that Lamartine, Cousin, Spinoza, and Plato were all noted pantheists and not Pan-worshipers gives him away. Lévi reinterprets Pan (the god of "all") as a personification of pantheism ("all is god") to connect this concept with Baphomet. The astral light, the spiritual force that pervades the entire universe, is pantheistic in nature, and thus it is not surprising that Lévi describes the Baphomet image as"a pantheistic and magical figure of the Absolute."[32]

Regarding the Baphomet of the Templars, as made evident in the quote above, Lévi did not judge them for supposedly worshiping Baphomet. To him, the great crime of the Templars was that "they have exposed to profane eyes the sanctuary of antique initiation."[33] Lévi often remarked on how adepts used bizarre or offensive images

31. Lévi, *Transcendental Magic*, 307–08.
32. Lévi, *Transcendental Magic*, xiv.
33. Lévi, *Transcendental Magic*, 8.

to hide sacred mysteries, thus was the monstrous appearance of Baphomet meant to conceal the mysteries it contains from those not ready to understand or use them. The takeaway here is that the Baphomet of the Templars was a symbol of ancient mysteries that the Catholic Church mistook for a satanic idol.

This same concept also applies to the title Goat of the Sabbath. In the introduction to *Doctrine and Ritual*, Lévi presents a sensationalized vision of the stereotypical Sabbath rite in which a goat-headed figure appears:

> We are in a landscape of Salvator Rosa, a troubled wilderness which seems resting after a storm. There is no moon in the sky, but you can distinguish little stars gleaming in the brushwood, and may hear about you the slow flight of great birds, which seem to whisper strange oracles as they pass. Let us approach silently that cross-road among the rocks. A harsh, funereal trumpet winds suddenly, and black torches flare up on every side. A tumultuous throng is surging round a vacant throne: all watch and wait. Suddenly they cast themselves on the ground. A goat-headed prince bounds forward among them; he ascends the throne, turns, and assuming a stooping posture, presents to the assembly a human face, which everyone comes forward to salute and to kiss, their black tapers in their hands. With a hoarse laugh he recovers an upright position, and then distributes gold, secret instructions, occult medicines and poisons to his faithful bondsmen. Meanwhile, fires are lighted of fern and alder, piled up with human bones and the fat of executed criminals. Druidesses, crowned with wild parsley and vervain,

> immolate unbaptised children with golden knives and prepare horrible love-feasts.[34]

After the banquet, everyone is drunk and starting to hallucinate, and then the men drag the women off into the darkness to have wild sex as the vision ends. But that's not what *really* happened! In chapter 15, "The Sabbath of the Sorcerers," Lévi presents a more erudite and esoteric explanation for the rites of the Sabbath:

> When Christianity proscribed the public exercise of the ancient worships, the partisans of the latter were compelled to meet in secret for the celebration of their mysteries. Initiates presided over these assemblies and soon established a kind of orthodoxy among the varieties of persecuted worships, this being facilitated by the aid of magical truth and by the fact that proscription unites wills and forges bonds of brotherhood between men. Thus, the Mysteries of Isis, of Ceres Eleusinia, of Bacchus, combined with those of the *Bona Dea* and primeval Druidism. The meetings took place usually between the days of Mercury and Jupiter, or between those of Venus and Saturn. The proceedings included Rites of Initiation, exchange of mysterious signs, singing of symbolical hymns, the communion of feasting in common, the successive formation of the magical chain at table and in the dance. Finally the meeting broke up after renewing pledges in the presence of chiefs and receiving instructions from them. The candidate for the Sabbath was led or rather carried to the assembly, his eyes covered by the magical mantle in which he was enveloped completely.

34. Lévi, *Transcendental Magic*, 6–7.

> He was passed before great fires, while alarming noises were made about him. When his face was uncovered, he found himself surrounded by infernal monsters and in the presence of a colossal and hideous goat which he was commanded to adore. All these ceremonies were tests of his force of character and confidence in his initiators. The final ordeal was most decisive of all because it was at first sight humiliating and ridiculous to the mind. The candidate received a brusque command to kiss respectfully the posterior of the goat. If he refused, his head was covered once more, and he was transported to a distance from the assembly with such extraordinary rapidity that he believed himself whirled through the air. If he agreed, he was taken round the symbolical idol, and there found, not a repulsive and obscene object, but the young and gracious countenance of a priestess of Isis or Maia, who gave him a sisterly salute, and he was then admitted to the banquet.[35]

No wild sex after *this* banquet. Keep in mind that Lévi's second account is about as fantastic as the first, for there is no evidence that such rites occurred during the Middle Ages when rumors of the sabbatic rite arose. Lévi surmised that like the Templars, the sabbath celebrants were practicing rites of the ancient mysteries that were misinterpreted as Satanic rituals.

To summarize, Baphomet as the Goat of Mendes is connected to the mysteries of the ancient Egyptians and ancient Greeks. As a representation of the astral light, Baphomet is pantheistic, linking Them to a belief shared by both the ancient schools and modern

35. Lévi, *Transcendental Magic*, 312–13.

philosophers. Finally, like the Baphomet of the Templars and the Goat of the Sabbath, the seemingly diabolical goat-headed image of Lévi's Baphomet is actually a façade to repel the profane from the sacred mysteries They represent. This is the most likely reason for using the goat's head and feet in his image: to use a Satanic symbol to conceal an icon of occult truth.

Trouble with Templars

In *Doctrine and Ritual,* Lévi mentions a third influence on his Baphomet image:

> A sculpted coffer was disinterred recently in the ruins of an old Commandery of the Temple, and antiquaries observed upon it a baphometic figure, corresponding by its attributes to the goat of Mendes and the androgyne of Khunrath. It was a bearded figure with a female body, holding the sun in one hand and the moon in the other, attached to chains. Now, this virile head is a beautiful allegory which attributes to thought alone the initiative and creative principle. Here the head represents spirit and the body matter. The orbs enchained to the human form, and directed by that Nature of which intelligence is the head, are also magnificently allegorical.[36]

36. Lévi, *Transcendental Magic*, 316.

Hammer-Purgstall's Androgyne

Unfortunately, the source of this image was Hammer-Purgstall's spurious essay "The Mysteries of Baphomet Revealed." Lévi remarks that this image "was discovered to be obscene and diabolical by the learned men that examined it,"[37] which alludes to Hammer-Purgstall's efforts to demonize the Templars. Still, it appears that Lévi accepted "The Mysteries" as an academic resource. It is even possible that Hammer-Purgstall's essay may have influenced Lévi's statements that connect Baphomet with the Gnostics.

37. Lévi, *Transcendental Magic*, 316.

While Lévi held a relatively favorable view of the Templars in *Doctrine and Ritual*, five years later, in *The History of Magic*, he changed his tune. Lévi accuses the Templars of pursuing a "terrible conspiracy" against the monarchs of Europe and the Catholic Church that involved securing the Holy Land for the Eastern Orthodox Church. He claimed that the Templars secretly adhered to the doctrine of Johannism, a pseudo-Christian tradition inherited from the Gnostics and based on the works and ideas of St. John the Evangelist, the author of the Book of Revelations. His strange and judgmental account of the Templars draws heavily from the works of Hammer-Purgstall and Barruel; Lévi even repeats Barruel's claim that the imprisoned Jacques de Molay established four Masonic lodges before he was executed.

Baphomet is mentioned only once in Lévi's sordid history of the Templars:

> They came to recognize the pantheistic symbolism of the great masters of Black Magic, and the better to isolate themselves from obedience to the religion which had already condemned them, they rendered divine honors to the monstrous idol Baphomet, even as of old the dissenting tribes had adored the Golden Calf of Dan and Bethel. Certain monuments of recent discovery and certain precious documents belonging to the thirteenth century offer abundant proof of all that is advanced here. Other evidences are concealed in the annals and beneath the symbols of Occult Masonry.[38]

Taken in context with his discussions of the Templars in other books, the true occult history of the Templars according to Lévi becomes clearer. The Templars originally possessed elements of

38. Lévi, *History of Magic*, 211.

ancient wisdom that may have been symbolized by Baphomet. But the Templars soon became corrupted by wealth, power, politics, and heresy; their wisdom was diluted or forgotten, and they began to idolize Baphomet. Proof of this corruption was found in "certain monuments of recent discovery" and "precious documents" from the Hammer-Purgstall essay. In the end, Lévi found the Templars guilty of corruption and heresy and thus lawfully prosecuted by the king and the pope.

Lévi's poor opinion of the Templars did not stop him from briefly joining the Masons in 1861. His friends initiated him into the Rose of Perfect Silence Lodge, where Lévi was made a Master Mason. However, Lévi wasn't impressed by the experience—he believed that the Masons didn't understand the occult significance of the symbols in their rituals and resigned from the Lodge by the end of the year.

The Tarot Connection

Lévi's system of magic is based on an extensive series of correspondences between the Qabala and the tarot. While he was not the first to make the connection between the twenty-two tarot trumps (major arcana) and the twenty-two letters of the Hebrew alphabet, Lévi was the first to develop these correspondences and incorporate them into Western esotericism. He fervently believed that these correspondences were the keys to the secrets of the ancient mysteries. Lévi weaved this belief into the structure of his magnum opus—*Doctrine* and *Ritual* are both divided into twenty-two chapters, as mentioned earlier, and each chapter in *Doctrine* is assigned a Hebrew letter. Many chapters in both parts of the book give descriptions of corresponding tarot trumps, including Chapter XV, "The Sabbath of the Sorcerers," which begins with a description of the Devil trump of the Marseilles Tarot:

The Devil Trump from the Marseilles Tarot

We recur once more to that terrible number fifteen, symbolized in the Tarot by a monster throned upon an altar, mitered and horned, having a woman's breasts and the generative organs of a man—a chimera, a malformed sphinx, a synthesis of deformities. Below this figure we can read a frank and simple inscription—THE DEVIL.[39]

39. Lévi, *Transcendental Magic*, 307.

The Devil trump of the Marseilles tarot was one of the primary influences upon Lévi's Baphomet image. He continues:

> Yes, we confront here that phantom of all terrors, the dragon of all theogonies, the Ahriman of the Persians, the Typhon of the Egyptians, the Python of the Greeks, the old serpent of the Hebrews, the fantastic monster, the nightmare, the Croquemitaine, the gargoyle, the great beast of the Middle Ages, and—worse than all these—the Baphomet of the Templars, the bearded idol of the alchemist, the obscene deity of Mendes, the goat of the Sabbath. The frontispiece to this "Ritual" reproduces the exact figure of the terrible emperor of night, with all his attributes and all his characters.[40]

While Lévi appears to be talking about the devil as an entity, other signs indicate the image of Baphomet was Lévi's rectified rendition of the Devil trump. When Lévi describes the images of tarot trumps at the end of *Doctrine and Ritual*, Baphomet appears: "Hieroglyph, THE DEVIL, the Goat of Mendes, or the Baphomet of the Temple, with all his pantheistic attributes."[41]

His interpretation of the Devil trump is different from other early French authors on the subject. While they indicate the influence of the Greek monster Typhon, "the spirit of catastrophes" representative of fatality, Lévi interprets the Devil as "the heaven of Mercury, occult science, Magic, commerce, eloquence, mystery, moral force."[42] It's not surprising that Baphomet, icon of the astral light and Azoth, would signify occult science, magic, and mystery; the rest of the interpretations are traditional attributions

---

40. Lévi, *Transcendental Magic*, 307.
41. Lévi, *Transcendental Magic*, 391.
42. Lévi, *Transcendental Magic*, 391.

of the planet Mercury and have little to do with the traditional imagery or interpretation of the Devil trump.

There were also rumors that Lévi drew up his own tarot deck. In 1861, Kenneth MacKenzie visited Lévi at his home in Paris, where he reported that Lévi had drawn up a complete set of tarot trumps:

> I said that I had been, for some time, making collections in reference to the occult game of Tarot, and that I wished particularly to learn whether he proposed to carry out the intention expressed in the "Rituel et Dogme de la Haute Magie" of issuing a complete set of Tarot cards.
>
> He replied that he was very willing to do so — and took from among his manuscripts a small volume in which were depicted the twenty-one cards of the Tarot with the Zero or Fool, according to the earliest authorities. Those cards were drawn by his own hand, and the little volume contained a large number of the symbols of Theurgia and Goetia, a medley of collections from the Key of Rabbi Solomon and similar occult repertories.
>
> This little work (he told me) had cost him twenty years to put together. He was kind enough to state that if I had any intention of publishing, in England, any set of Tarot cards, I might count upon him for all assistance, and that he would supply me with all drawings and instructions for their use.[43]

Unfortunately, Lévi's tarot trumps or any other sign of a redrawn tarot deck were not discovered after his death, leaving us with only the two trump illustrations from *Doctrine and Ritual*,

---

43. Christopher McIntosh, *Éliphas Lévi and the French Occult Revival* (State University of New York, 2011), 118.

Baphomet/the Devil and the Chariot. On the other hand, the connection between Lévi's Baphomet and the Devil trump lived on in the works and the tarot decks of the next generation of occultists.

Lévi's Tarot Legacy

One person inspired by Lévi's work was Swiss occultist and Freemason Oswald Wirth. In 1889, under the guidance of his mentor, French poet and occultist Stanislas de Guaita (another of Lévi's spiritual heirs), Wirth published *The Kabalistic Tarot*, a cartomantic deck featuring the twenty-two major arcana. The Devil trump of this deck resembles Lévi's Baphomet, a goat-man hybrid with arms inscribed with *solve* and *coagula* and the sigil of Mercury over the genital area. However, Wirth's image has a more sinister tone, with a devilish face and bat wings; the upright pentagram is gone and it holds a torch in its right hand and a lamp in its left. In *The Tarot of the Magicians*, published in 1927, Wirth pays homage to Éliphas Lévi and discusses the Kabalistic keys found in Lévi's *Doctrine and Ritual*. In the entry on the Devil trump, Wirth talks about the Baphomet connection; his explanation of the symbolism relies heavily on Lévi.

Wirth's deck had a strong influence on English occult scholar and Freemason Arthur Edward Waite, who published the quintessential Rider-Waite-Smith Tarot in 1910. Waite's Devil bears the same devilish face and bat wings as Wirth's trump, but Waite's version is even more Satanic. This Devil has an inverted pentagram on its forehead, holds the torch of intelligence upside-down in its left hand, and raises and extends its right hand bearing the sigil of Saturn on its palm—all signs of misfortune and evil.

The Devil Trump from the Rider-Waite-Smith Tarot

In *The Pictorial Key to the Tarot*, Waite identifies the Devil with the Goat of Mendes, then takes a swipe at Lévi:

> With more than his usual derision for the arts which he pretended to respect and interpret as a master therein, Éliphas Lévi affirms the Baphometic figure is occult science and magic. . . . What it does signify is the Dweller on the Threshold without the mystical garden when

> those are driven forth therefrom who have eaten the forbidden fruit.[44]

The Waite-Smith Tarot has become one of the most influential and popular tarot decks in the world, and its art and symbols have been imitated and modified by many generations of tarot artists creating their own decks, including Waite's Satan/Baphomet hybrid. Many stay true to Waite's design, but a few artists restore the figure of Baphomet to its full glory, often in recognition of Lévi's contributions to the occult tarot.

Baphomet Is Not Satan!

The one thing that Lévi's Baphomet did not represent was Satan. We know this for a fact because, first of all, Lévi didn't believe in Satan! He states this many times in *Doctrine and Ritual*:

> Let us affirm categorically, to combat the remnants of Manichaenism which are appearing sporadically among Christians, that as a superior personality and power Satan does not exist. He is the personification of all errors, perversities and consequently of all weaknesses. If God may be defined as He Who exists of necessity, may we not define His antagonist and enemy as necessarily he who does not exist at all?[45]

Again, in more forceful words:

> Get thee behind us, Satan! We renounce thee, with all thy pomps and works, and still more with all thy deformities,

44. Arthur Edward Waite, *The Pictorial Key to the Tarot* (Causeway, 1973; originally published 1910 by William Rider & Sons), 128–31.
45. Lévi, *Transcendental Magic*, 310.

> thy meanness, thy nothingness, thy deception! The Great Initiator beheld thee fall from heaven like a thunderbolt. The Christian legend changes thee, making thee set thy dragon's head mildly beneath the foot of the Mother of God. Thou art for us the image of unintelligence and mystery; thou art unreason and blind fanaticism; thou art the inquisition and its hell; thou art the god of Torquemada and Alexander VI; thou hast become the sport of children, and thy final resting place is at the side of Polichinello. Henceforth, thou art only a grotesque figure in our travelling booths and a means of instruction in a few so-called religious markets.[46]

Lévi also made it clear that Baphomet is not an image of Satan. After explaining the symbolism of the Baphomet image in "The Sabbath of the Sorcerers," Lévi declares that the sinister mystery of Baphomet has been dispelled: "The dread Baphomet henceforth, like all monstrous idols, enigmas of antique science and its dreams, is only an innocent and even pious hieroglyph."[47] He also states that the upright pentagram on Baphomet's forehead "stops one from taking him for a fabulous image of Satan."[48]

Finally, it is important to understand that Lévi did not consider Baphomet to be a representation of *any* living or spiritual being. In *The Book of Splendors*, one of the last books written before his death, Lévi declares that Baphomet "is knowledge rising in opposition to idolatry, protesting through the very monstrosity of the idol." He then likens Baphomet with the cherubs on the Ark of the Covenant:

---

46. Lévi, *Transcendental Magic*, 333.
47. Lévi, *Transcendental Magic*, 310.
48. Lévi, *Doctrine and Ritual*, 318.

> The Israelites were forbidden to give divine concepts the figure of man or of any animal; thus, on the Ark of the Covenant, they dared sculpt only cherubs, that is, sphinxes with the bodies of bulls and the heads of men, eagles, or lions.
>
> These hybrid creatures of impossible animals gave to understand that the image was not an idol or reproduction of a living thing, but rather a character or representation of something having its existence in thought.
>
> Baphomet is not worshiped; it is God who is worshiped, the faceless God behind this formless form, this image which resembles no created being.
>
> Baphomet is not God: he is a sign of initiation.[49]

For the record: Éliphas Lévi, the creator of Baphomet, did not believe in Satan, did not believe that his Baphomet represented Satan, and did not even believe in Baphomet as a spiritual entity.

Éliphas Lévi was the modern creator of Baphomet. His drawing defines the physical characteristics of the deity: a goat's head with a flaming torch between its horns and a pentagram on its forehead, placed on a winged androgynous body, with symbolic genitalia, sitting upon a cube; its right arm, inscribed with the word *solve*, points upward, and its left arm, inscribed with *coagula*, points downward in what has become known as the attitude or pose of Baphomet.

To Lévi, Baphomet represented the harmonious expression of the astral light and Azoth, both analogous with the element

49. Lévi, *The Book of Splendours* (Samuel Weiser, 1984), 118.

of spirit. The androgynous body alludes to the combination of masculine and feminine energies in alchemy, and it also represents the economic, sexual, and spiritual harmony that would manifest within a socialist utopia. Lévi connects Baphomet to the ancient mysteries of the Egyptians and Greeks and concludes that the Templars originally possessed knowledge of these mysteries but lost them when they became corrupted by wealth and power, whereupon they started worshiping Baphomet. Finally, Lévi links Baphomet to the Devil trump in the major arcana but denies any link between Baphomet and Satan. Lévi's conception of Baphomet serves as the foundation upon which all other conceptions are built.

XV
ע The Devil
XV
XV
THE DEVIL.

Chapter 3
Baphomet and the Beast

The works of Éliphas Lévi helped spark an occult revival in America and Europe, particularly in France and England. Occultists of the late nineteenth and early twentieth centuries incorporated many of Lévi's ideas into new magical systems, but Baphomet—if mentioned at all—was only discussed in the context of the symbolism of the Devil trump.

But in 1875, six months after Éliphas Lévi died, his soul crossed the English Channel and was reincarnated as Edward Alexander Crowley, or so the latter claimed. While this intimate connection may have only been real in Crowley's mind, there is no doubt that Lévi was a significant influence on the life and works of Crowley, especially regarding Baphomet.

Enter Aleister Crowley

Edward Alexander Crowley was born into a wealthy family in Leamington Spa, Warwickshire, England. Members of a fundamentalist sect known as the Plymouth Brethren, his family did not celebrate traditional Christian holidays and strictly limited who Crowley could associate with and what the young boy could read (other than the Bible).

When young Crowley misbehaved, his mother would call him the Great Beast 666, a satanic appellation that would prove oddly fitting in later years. As he grew older, he rejected and despised the religion of his childhood. During his time at Cambridge, Crowley started to identify himself as Aleister, the Gaelic version of Alexander.

In 1897, Crowley developed an interest in the occult that led him to join the Hermetic Order of the Golden Dawn, an initiatory magical group, a year later. It was there that Crowley got his basic education in Western esotericism, studying magical rituals, tarot, astrology, alchemy, and western Qabala. After leaving the Golden Dawn, he went to India to study Buddhism and Hindu yoga.

The defining moment of Crowley's life came in 1904 with his reception of *The Book of the Law*. The three chapters of this holy book contained strange revelations from three deities: Nuit, Hadit, and Ra-Hoor-Khuit, each proclaiming the advent of a New Aeon of spiritual evolution. Identified in *The Book of the Law* by his childhood nickname "the Beast," Crowley was chosen as prophet and priest of the new religion, Thelema, in the dawning New Aeon of Horus. It became Crowley's mission to promote Thelema as the religion of the New Aeon, to bring people to the discovery and accomplishment of their true wills, and to free them from the restrictive bonds of the previous Old Aeon of Osiris.

In 1907, Crowley and his former Golden Dawn mentor, George Cecil Jones, formed the A∴A∴, a magical order dedicated to individual instruction and attainment that incorporated the religion and philosophy of Thelema. Crowley never publicly revealed what the initials A∴A∴ stood for; the most common definition is *Astrum Argentum*, Latin for "silver star." From 1909 to 1913, they published *The Equinox*, the official journal of the A∴A∴, wherein Crowley and his colleagues contributed articles about magic and

Aleister Crowley as Baphomet X°

mysticism as well as poems, plays, reviews, and fiction. Also, 1909 was the year that Crowley first published *The Book of the Law*.

In 1912, German occultist Theodor Reuss, head of the Ordo Templi Orientis (O.T.O.), confronted Crowley and accused him of revealing the Order's most valuable secret, a special technique of sex magic, in a recently published book. When Crowley realized the significance of what he had written, Reuss had to initiate him into the O.T.O. to safeguard the Order's secret. Reuss made Crowley the head of the British O.T.O.; within the order, Crowley took Baphomet as his magical name.

Latin for the "Order of Oriental Templars" or "Order of the Temple of the East," the Ordo Templi Orientis is a fraternal occult initiatory organization founded at the beginning of the twentieth century by Austrian industrialist Carl Kellner and Theodor Reuss. At the core of the O.T.O.'s instruction and initiation is a powerful technique of sexual magic commonly known as the Ninth Degree secret, so-called because it is only fully revealed to initiates of the Ninth Degree, the highest level of initiation in the O.T.O. The revelation of the Ninth Degree secret to Crowley was a watershed moment in his life. Sex magic soon became his preferred method of magical working. Crowley was bisexual and performed sex magic operations and experiments with both men and women for the remainder of his life.

After Reuss died in 1923, Crowley became the head of the entire O.T.O., which served as both his primary vehicle for promoting the religion of Thelema and as a source of much-needed income. At the end of the decade, he published his magnum opus on occultism, *Magick in Theory and Practice*. Like Lévi's *Doctrine and Ritual of High Magic*, Crowley's work had twenty-two chapters. In it, he presents evidence that he was Éliphas Lévi in his previous incarnation. During his lifetime, Crowley published a number of influential books on magic and Thelema, including *Liber Aleph*, a series of letters and instructions written for his magical son; *777*, a compendium of qabalistic and hermetic correspondences; *The Holy Books of Thelema*, a collection of received or inspired works related to Thelema; and *The Equinox of the Gods*, which told the story behind the reception of *The Book of the Law*.

The last major project of Crowley's life involved collaborating with artist Lady Frieda Harris to create the Thoth tarot. The two worked for five years to produce an updated deck that incorporated symbols and concepts from Thelema and sex magic. He published the companion book for the deck, *The Book of Thoth*, in 1944, but the deck remained unpublished when Crowley died of acute bronchitis in 1947. The Thoth tarot was finally published over two decades later, and it soon became one of the most popular decks in the world.

Baphomet Speaks

Crowley's first major work that mentions Baphomet, *Liber A'ash*, originally appeared in *The Equinox*, vol. 1, no. 6 in the spring of 1911. The text's full name is *Liber A'ash vel Capricorni Pneumatici*, which translates to "The Book of Creation or of the Goat of the Spirit." *Liber A'ash* is one of the Holy Books of Thelema, books of magical and mystical instruction integral to the development and practice of Thelema. Crowley cataloged *Liber A'ash* as a Class A document, meaning the text "may be changed not so much as the style of a letter" because it was "channeled" or "inspired." Class A documents were usually received in a trance, and sometimes even Crowley didn't fully comprehend their meaning.

Liber A'ash "analyzes the nature of the creative force in man, explains how to awaken it, how to use it and indicates the general as well as the particular object to be obtained thereby."[50] The first part of the document presents a technique of sex magic veiled in allegory; then Baphomet introduces Themselves:

> 17. Now shalt thou adore me who am the Eye and the Tooth, the Goat of the Spirit, the Lord of Creation. I am the Eye in the Triangle, the Silver Star that ye adore.
>
> 18. I am Baphomet, that is the Eightfold Word that shall be equilibrated with the Three.
>
> 19. There is no act or passion that shall not be a hymn in mine honour.
>
> 20. All holy things and all symbolic things shall be my sacraments.[51]

This introduction is extremely significant—this is the first time Baphomet manifests as an actual spiritual entity as opposed to an esoteric icon or a satanic symbol. In one sense, these are Baphomet's first words! It also implies that Baphomet dictated *Liber A'ash* to Crowley, suggesting Baphomet might have a role to play in Thelema. Unfortunately, a full analysis of *Liber A'ash* would require much more space, perhaps its own chapter. However, most of the verses deal largely with sex magic, Thelemic deities, and other Thelemic concepts that would do little to advance our understanding of Crowley's conception of Baphomet.

---

50. Aleister Crowley, *The Confessions of Aleister Crowley*, eds. John Symonds and Kenneth Grant (Arkana, 1989), 674.
51. Aleister Crowley, *The Equinox* 1, no. 6 (1911): 23.

One might wonder if receiving *Liber A'ash* influenced Crowley's decision to take the magical name of Baphomet when he was appointed as the "Supreme and Holy King of Ireland, Ionia, and all the Britains within the Sanctuary of the Gnosis" of the O.T.O. a year later. Crowley biographer Laurence Sutin suggests that multiple factors were involved in the decision for Crowley to administrate the O.T.O. as Baphomet. The head of the O.T.O. at the time, Theodore Reuss, probably had a say in naming Crowley Baphomet. Sutin reports that "Baphomet lore was regarded by Reuss as crucial to the great secret of the O.T.O.," which suggests that the androgynous Baphomet had something to do with the Ninth Degree secret.[52] Indeed, one of the Seventh Degree papers reveals that the Templars met with Islamic initiates who taught them a secret called Baphomet. Everything suggests that Baphomet was an important symbol in the O.T.O. before Crowley became involved.

Baphomet also had a great deal of significance to Crowley, who claimed to have created the original Baphomet image in his previous incarnation as Éliphas Lévi:

> Now the Path of Ayin ... in the Zodiac importeth the Goat. This Goat is called also Strength, and standeth in the Meridian at the Sunrise of Spring; and it is His Nature to leap upon the Mountains. So therefore he is a Symbol of true Magick, and his Name is Baphomet, wherefore did I design him as an Atu of Thoth, the Fifteenth, and put his Image in the Front of my Book, the "Ritual of High Magick", which was the second Part of my Thesis

52. Laurence Sutin, *Do What Thou Wilt: A Life of Aleister Crowley* (St. Martin's, 2000), 226.

> for the Grade of Major Adept, when I was clothed about with the Body called Alphonse Louis Constant.[53]

For those unfamiliar with the occult correspondences in the first two sentences, the fifteenth tarot trump, the Devil, is associated with the Hebrew letter *Ayin* and the zodiacal sign Capricorn; the Hebrew word for "goat," *oz*, also means "strength"; finally, the Sun is in Capricorn from December 21 to January 21, after the winter solstice when the days get longer and the earth begins to warm, heralding the upcoming spring.

Incidentally, there is some confusion within Crowley's works concerning the nature of Baphomet's head. In most instances Crowley goes with Lévi's traditional goat head, but sometimes he refers to Baphomet as an ass-headed god to connect Them with Set and Satan.

Yet, Crowley clearly did not believe in Satan. While he had been labeled a Satanist in the press and the pulpit, he never worked with the Christian devil, whom he considered a relic of the previous Aeon of Osiris. In *Magick in Theory and Practice*, Crowley declared, "The Devil does not exist."

> "The Devil" is, historically, the God of any people that one personally dislikes. This has led to so much confusion that THE BEAST 666 has preferred to let names stand as they are, and to proclaim that AIWAZ—the solar-phallic-hermetic "Lucifer"—is His own Holy Guardian Angel, and "The Devil" SATAN or HADIT, the supreme soul behind RA-HOOR-KHUIT the Sun, the Lord of our particular unit of the Starry Universe. This serpent, SATAN,

---

53. Aleister Crowley, *Liber Aleph vel CXI: The Book of Wisdom or Folly* (Samuel Weiser, 1991), 174.

> is not the enemy of Man, but He who made Gods of our race, knowing Good and Evil; He bade "Know Thyself!" and taught Initiation. He is "The Devil" of the Book of Thoth, and His emblem is BAPHOMET, the Androgyne who is the hieroglyph of arcane perfection.[54]

As such, Crowley redefined Satan in a positive sense that fit into his understanding of the universe. He incorporated the old Aeon concept of the devil into Thelema by identifying Satan with Hadit, the new Aeon deity revealed in the second chapter of *The Book of the Law*. He also associates Hadit with the serpent of Genesis and Baphomet, both symbols of Satan in the Old Aeon.

The Mass of Baphomet

Despite the Templar theme of the O.T.O., Baphomet does not appear in any of its initiation rituals. However, Baphomet does play a special role in one of Crowley's most celebrated rituals, the Gnostic Mass. The Gnostic Mass is a eucharistic ritual based on the masses of the Roman Catholic Church and the Eastern Orthodox Church but updated to reflect the Law of Thelema and the philosophy of the New Aeon of Horus. It was written in 1913, around the time when Baphomet first became significant in Crowley's life, but wasn't published until 1918, and the first public performance of the Mass in 1933 didn't involve Crowley at all. Nonetheless, the Gnostic Mass became the primary public ritual of the O.T.O., and today all established O.T.O. bodies are required to perform it on a regular basis.

While allusions to Baphomet can be found in many parts of the Gnostic Mass, Their actual name only appears in the creed. In the context of the Roman Catholic Mass, the creed is a statement

54. Aleister Crowley, *Liber ABA* (Samuel Weiser, 2000), 277.

of belief in the Gospel of Jesus and the doctrine of the church recited by the congregation. Crowley cleverly placed his creed at the beginning of the Gnostic Mass so that the congregation must declare their belief in the deities and concepts that make the Mass work as a magical ritual:

> I believe in one secret and ineffable LORD; and in one Star in the Company of Stars of whose fire we are created, and to which we shall return; and in one Father of Life, Mystery of Mystery, in His name CHAOS, the sole vicegerent of the Sun upon the Earth; and in one Air, the nourisher of all that breathes.
>
> And I believe in one Earth, the Mother of us all, and in one Womb wherein all men are begotten, and wherein they shall rest, Mystery of Mystery, in Her name BABALON.
>
> And I believe in the Serpent and the Lion, Mystery of Mystery, in His name BAPHOMET.
>
> And I believe in one Gnostic and Catholic Church of Light, Life, Love and Liberty, the Word of whose Law is THELEMA.
>
> And I believe in the communion of Saints.
>
> And, forasmuch as meat and drink are transmuted in us daily into spiritual substance, I believe in the Miracle of the Mass.
>
> And I confess one Baptism of Wisdom whereby we accomplish the Miracle of Incarnation.
>
> And I confess my life one, individual, and eternal that was, and is, and is to come.[55]

55. Aleister Crowley, *The Equinox* 3, no. 1 (1919): 251–52.

In order to understand the meaning of Baphomet in the context of the creed, you have to look at the Gnostic Mass from a different perspective. It turns out that the Gnostic Mass also enacts the Ninth Degree secret of sex magic in allegorical form. Sex magic takes the significant amount of energy released by orgasm and harnesses it to obtain a desired result. Sex magic between a man and a woman is considered particularly potent because together they have the potential to perform the "Miracle of Incarnation" and bring a new life into the world. The combined sexual fluids of the male and female are considered to be charged with the energy and purpose of the sex magic operation, so they are often consumed after orgasm.

In the Gnostic Mass, the priest and priestess symbolically enact this technique of sex magic and use it to empower the sacraments of the Mass, the host and the wine. The priest gets spiritual aid from the god Chaos, the "one Father of Life," the divine masculine archetype; the priestess is assisted by Babalon, "the Mother of us all," the divine feminine archetype. At the climax of the Mass, the priest and priestess plunge his Sacred Lance (the phallus) into her Cup (the womb) while saying "Hriliu," a word described as "the shrill scream of orgasm." The result of this union is Baphomet, the androgyne symbolic of the creative energy of the male and female present in the combined sexual fluids. On a spiritual level, Baphomet is the magical child of Chaos and Babalon. As indicated in the Creed, Baphomet is the "Baptism of Wisdom"—Hammer-Purgstall's definition of the name Baphomet—"whereby we accomplish the Miracle of Incarnation."

The Creed defines Baphomet as "the Serpent and the Lion," more commonly known in Crowley's works as the lion-serpent. The key to understanding the lion-serpent is the Hebrew letter Teth, which means "serpent" when spelled in full and is attributed to Leo the lion in the zodiac. Specifically, the lion-serpent is the sperm, represented by a serpent with the head of a lion; on a general level, the lion-serpent represents the creative power in all humans. By associating Them with the lion-serpent, Crowley has truly made Baphomet the "Lord of Creation" as proclaimed in *Liber A'ash*.

After the climax of the Mass, the priest strikes his breast and says, "O Lion and O Serpent that destroy the destroyer, be mighty among us!"[56] three times. In this action, he acknowledges that Baphomet, the lion-serpent, is now present. The destroyer is death, and that which destroys the destroyer is the creation of new life, the creative force known as Baphomet. The priest and the congregation then take communion, the sacraments infused with the energy of Baphomet.

Crowley's Gnostic Mass symbolically associates Baphomet with the creative force of sex magic. This is reminiscent of and probably related to Lévi's original concept of Baphomet as a representation of the astral light. Both authors saw Baphomet as the means by which magic was accomplished, but while Lévi saw Baphomet as a symbol, Crowley treats Them like a spiritual entity and even gives Them divine parents.

The Tarot Reconnection

The vast web of correspondences created by Lévi's marriage of the Qabala, magic, and the tarot were integrated into the Golden Dawn system of magic. Crowley memorized these correspondences during his time in the Golden Dawn and used them as a foundation for his own system of Thelema. However, Crowley soon realized that he would have to change a few things to make

---

56. Crowley, *The Equinox* 3, 268.

the old Golden Dawn correspondences more relevant in the New Aeon of Horus; one of those things was to determine where Baphomet really belonged in the tarot.

In his early works, Crowley usually mentions Baphomet in the context of Their traditional correspondences with the Devil trump, the Hebrew letter Ayin, and the zodiacal sign Capricorn.[57] The connection Lévi created between the Devil trump and Baphomet had been firmly established at the beginning of the twentieth century with the publication of the popular Rider-Waite-Smith tarot deck, which features the Devil trump with the sinister Baphomet image described in chapter 2. Crowley was simply following the lead of what he believed was his previous incarnation.

However, Crowley's perspective on Baphomet changed as he matured—he started to focus less on the goat and devil symbolism and more on Baphomet's sexual nature. This is not a surprising development considering Crowley's earliest experiences with Baphomet revolve around sex magic. Baphomet may have been associated with the devil in the Old Aeon of Osiris, but They had a different role to play in the New Aeon of Horus.

In his later works, Crowley associates Baphomet with other bisexual or androgynous gods and the Hebrew letter Aleph, which corresponds to the Fool trump in the tarot. One of the first examples can be found in *Magick in Theory and Practice*:

> The quality of [Aleph] is ... bisexual. It is the original being—Zeus Arrhenothelus, Bacchus Diphues, or Baphomet.[58]

57. For example, see the quote from *Liber Aleph* on pages 73–74.
58. Crowley, *Liber ABA*, 171.

A similar example appears in commentary on *The Vision and the Voice*:

> The whole symbolism of *aleph*, 111, must be studied thoroughly. ... *Aleph* is Iacchus, Lord of Ecstasy; Harpocrates, Lord of Silence; Zeus Arrhenothelus; Bacchus Diphues; Baphomet, etc. Lord of the Two-in-One Love ...[59]

These examples make more sense if you take a closer look at the path of Aleph on the Qabalistic Tree of Life. The path of Aleph connects the sephiroth Kether and Chokmah, the first and second spheres of emanation. Aleph is much higher on the tree than the path of Ayin; in fact, Aleph is so high on the tree that it is above Chokmah and Binah, the sephiroth that establish gender in the universe. Therefore, deities and images attributed to Aleph are usually androgynous and hermaphroditic (for example, Zeus Arrhenothelus and Baphomet), or at least bisexual (for example, Bacchus Diphues). Aleph also receives the attribution of the element of air, which is traditionally understood as the union of fire (male) and water (female)—much like Baphomet at the end of the Gnostic Mass. Finally, the attribution of Baphomet to Aleph places Them next to Kether, the source of the universe, thus raising Baphomet to a much more divine status.

By the time we get to *The Book of Thoth*, Crowley's last major work, Baphomet is listed among the deities and traditions that influenced the symbolism of the Fool trump in the Thoth deck, along with Harpocrates, Zeus Arrhenothelus, and Bacchus Diphues. However, there is very little Baphomet-related symbolism

---

59. Aleister Crowley, *The Vision and the Voice with Commentary and Other Papers* (Samuel Weiser, 1998), footnote 77.

in the Fool image, and the few commonalities such as the horns and the androgynous figure are simply coincidental.

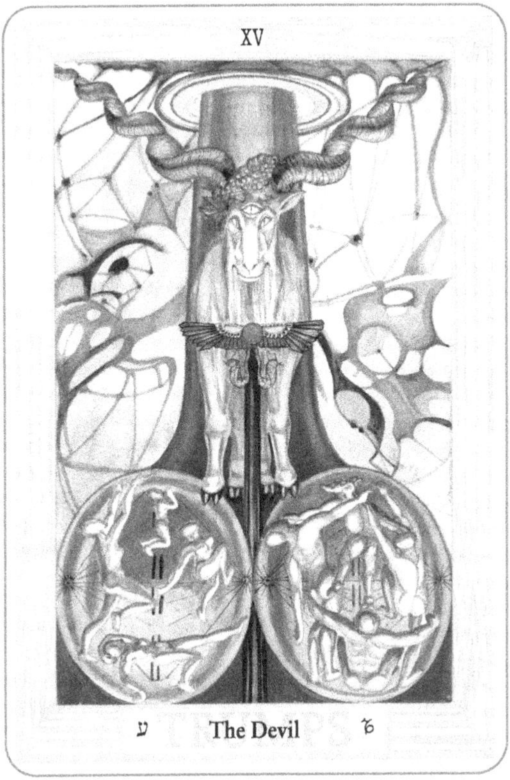

The Thoth Tarot Devil Card

In the section on the Devil trump, Crowley makes it clear that Baphomet has moved away and refers the reader back to the Fool trump. He credits Lévi for redefining the Devil trump with his image of Baphomet, but claims that "at this time archaeological research had not gone very far; the nature of Baphomet was not fully understood." Then Crowley accedes that "at least he succeeded in identifying the goat portrayed upon the card with Pan."[60] Crowley's Devil trump depicts a goat with a third eye and a bunch of grapes upon his head who "represents Pan Pangenitor, the All-Begetter" leaping "upon the highest and most secret mountains of the earth."[61]

It's interesting that Crowley's *Book of Thoth* mentions nothing about Baphomet's connection with sex magic, and ironic considering that, like the Gnostic Mass, the trumps of the Thoth tarot present the secrets of sex magic in symbolic form. In the context of the sexual symbolism of the cards, Baphomet would be attributed to the Art trump in the Thoth tarot, which shows the post-coital combination of male and female sexual fluids symbolized by an androgyne with two heads, a queen and a king, co-mingling the elements of fire and water.

Crowley's relationship with Baphomet was short. First, Baphomet contacted Crowley through *Liber A'ash*; then Crowley became known as Baphomet after inadvertently revealing the sex magic secret of a secret occult order; and finally, Crowley deified Baphomet by writing Them into the Gnostic Mass. After that, there is only a lingering, insubstantial link between Baphomet and Thelema and a connection with the Fool trump that never really materializes. Three years was all it took for Baphomet to get what They needed from Crowley.

60. Aleister Crowley, *The Book of Thoth* (Samuel Weiser, 1993), 105. Atu 0 is the Fool trump.

61. Crowley, *The Book of Thoth*, 105.

Crowley initiated the final stage in the evolution of Baphomet. Lévi gave Them form as an occult symbol, but it was in the works of Crowley that Baphomet actually became a deity. He was also the first person to explore the connection between Baphomet and human sexuality, a connection that became much more prominent in the twenty-first century.

Chapter 4

The Influence of Satan

After Crowley died in 1947, Baphomet faded from view. However, the rise of Neopaganism in the 1960s renewed interest in the works and ideas of Lévi and Crowley. New religious and spiritual groups started to develop their own ideas about the nature of Baphomet... but then the High Priest of Satan intervened.

When the founder of the Church of Satan created the Sigil of Baphomet to represent his newly formed religion, he linked Baphomet with Satan in mainstream America. This satanic connection deterred many Neopagan groups from working with the deity, especially because they were already fighting to distinguish themselves from Satanists in many Christian-majority countries. Half a century later, the political activities of the Satanic Temple have brought Baphomet back into the mainstream spotlight, helping to turn Baphomet into a popular culture icon and increasing interest in the deity in post-Christian society.

The O.T.O. Revival

At the time of Crowley's death, the O.T.O. had shrunk to one active body, Agapé Lodge in Pasadena, California. Crowley's successor, Karl Germer, had focused more on publishing Crowley's works than initiating new members, and he died in 1962 without naming a successor, leaving the O.T.O. on life support.

The resuscitation of the O.T.O. began in 1969, when one of Crowley's students, Grady McMurtry, took control of the O.T.O. and started initiating new members into the Order. In 1977, McMurtry founded Thelema Lodge in Berkeley, California, and the O.T.O. began chartering new groups in the United States and around the world. Thelema Lodge became the hub of the modern O.T.O.

The resurrected O.T.O. began an ambitious project to bring Crowley's major works back into regular publication. Innovations in book publishing and distribution meant that Crowley's works became easier and cheaper to obtain than they were during his lifetime and at a time when there was a surge of interest in Neopaganism and the occult. As a result, Crowley's works and ideas influenced many newly forming Neopagan and occult groups.

One might think that this significant Crowleyan influence on Neopaganism might have generated more interest in Baphomet in these emerging esoteric circles. However, one man influenced in part by Crowley installed Baphomet as the figurehead for his new "religion" of Satanism, a move that discouraged many Neopagan groups from developing their own relationship with the deity.

The Sigil of Baphomet

The Church of Satan was founded in 1966 by Anton Szandor LaVey. Their website proclaims that they are "the first above-ground organization in history openly dedicated to the acceptance of Man's true nature—that of a carnal beast, living in a cosmos that is indifferent to our existence."[62] Members do not consider Satan to be the evil supernatural entity of Christian mythology; in the Church of Satan, Satan "represents pride, liberty, and individualism."[63]

LaVey found the symbol for his new church on the cover of *A Pictorial History of Magic and the Supernatural* by Maurice Bessy. Bessy had adopted the symbol from *La Clef de la Magie Noire (The Key to Black Magic)* by French occultist Stanislas de Guaita. Neither Bessy nor de Guaita had associated this symbol with Baphomet.

Stanislas de Guaita's Pentacle
from the cover of *La Clef de la Magie Noire*

De Guaita's original image, which was displayed in Bessy's book, featured a goat's head drawn within a pentagram surrounded by two circles. In the interior circle, the names Samael

62. https://www.churchofsatan.com/.
63. https://www.churchofsatan.com/.

and Lilith are inscribed between the points of the pentagram, and between the interior and exterior circles the name Leviathan is inscribed in Hebrew.

De Guaita's image was inspired by Éliphas Lévi, who had described the pentagram in *The Key of the Mysteries*:

> The flaming star, which, when turned upside down, is the hieroglyphic sign of the goat of Black Magic, whose head may then be drawn in the star, the two horns at the top, the ears to the right and left, the beard at the bottom. It is the sign of antagonism and fatality. It is the goat of lust attacking the heavens with its horns. It is a sign execrated by initiates of a superior rank, even at the Sabbath.[64]

Lévi is the source of the idea that associates upright pentagrams (with one point up) with good and inverted pentagrams (two points up) with evil.

Bessy's cover featured a modified version of de Guaita's symbol, which was printed in white on a black background and omitted the names Lilith and Samael. This cover image became the prototype for the Sigil of Baphomet, the emblem of the Church of Satan; LaVey modified the image a year or two later, correcting the geometry of the circles and pentagram and redrawing the Hebrew letters and the goat, all with the intention of creating a unique sigil for the Church. The official Sigil of Baphomet made its public debut on the cover of *The Satanic Mass* LP in 1968, but the image didn't achieve widespread recognition until the publication of *The Satanic Bible* in 1969.

---

64. Lévi, *The Key of the Mysteries*, 112.

LaVey's Baphomet

The Satanic Bible defines Baphomet in the context of the Church of Satan:

> Baphomet represents the Powers of Darkness combined with the generative fertility of the goat. In its "pure" form the pentagram is shown encompassing the figure of a man in the five points of the star—three points up, two pointing down—symbolizing man's spiritual nature. In Satanism the pentagram is also used, but since Satanism represents the carnal instincts of man, or the opposite of the spiritual nature, the pentagram is inverted to perfectly accommodate the head of the goat—its horns, representing duality, thrust upwards in defiance; the other three points inverted, or the trinity denied. The Hebraic figures around the outer circle of the symbol which stem from the magical teachings of the Kabala, spell out "Leviathan," the serpent of the watery abyss, and identified with Satan. These figures correspond to the five points of the inverted star.[65]

The "Powers of Darkness" refer to the forces of nature, which create and destroy without joy or remorse.[66] The combination of the forces of nature with the generative fertility of the goat evoke ideas of energy, vitality, virility, and lust—fitting concepts for LaVey's carnal philosophy. The middle of the paragraph is mostly an elaboration of ideas from Lévi on the origin of the concept of good and evil pentagrams. Finally, while it is true that Leviathan is identified with Satan, the use of Hebrew letters and the reference

65. Anton Szandor LaVey, *The Satanic Bible* (Avon, 1969), 136.
66. LaVey, *The Satanic Bible*, 62.

to "the magical teachings of the Kabala" seems to be an odd choice for a man espousing a post-Christian philosophy.

There's nothing complicated about the symbolism of Baphomet in the Church of Satan; *The Satanic Bible* simply associates Baphomet with Satan. Unlike Lévi and Crowley, LaVey does not consider Baphomet to be an independent entity. In fact, in a letter to Michael Aquino, LaVey indicated that he didn't care much for the original Baphomet image:

> ... I felt Lévi's version, while luridly graphic for the 19th Century, is far too euphemistic for today's climate. Such concessions as the ill-fitted "good" pentagram on the forehead, the caduceus in lieu of a virile member, the lap robe to avoid exposure of the caduceus' point of origin, a rather unimaginative pair of 39 D-cup mammary glands, arms that would better serve in an ad for Jergen's lotion, a right hand in the act of hailing a cab, and a Roman candle perched atop the head do little to advance the impression of the truly base and carnal aspect of the Beast of the World![67]

As the trademarked icon of the Church of Satan, the Sigil of Baphomet is found everywhere within the organization. In rituals, the Sigil is placed on the wall above the altar, and Baphomet is one the Infernal Names of the forces of Darkness that one can invoke for assistance. The Sigil may be found on all official documents, books, and websites. Cloisonné medallions bearing the Sigil of Baphomet (initially given only to members but eventually offered

67. Michael A. Aquino, *The Satanic Bible: 50th Anniversary ReVision* (Self-published, 2018), 377.

to the public) became the primary means of identifying other Satanists in public.

The inverted pentagram and the Sigil of Baphomet were also adopted by the denizens of counterculture, particularly among heavy metal bands that emerged in the 1980s. Many artists employed these symbols along with other Satanic imagery for their shock value, using them in album cover art and in music videos, delighting rebellious teens and distressing their parents.

Furthermore, internal dissent within the Church of Satan prompted members to leave and form their own Satanic organizations, while the media hype around the Church of Satan encouraged other people to start their own theistic and nontheistic Satanic groups. In most cases, these Satanic organizations followed the trend set by LaVey and adopted Baphomet as a superficial symbol of Satan.

The appropriation of Baphomet by the Church of Satan in the late 1960s and the establishment of Baphomet as a Satanic symbol in popular culture soured Pagan interest in Baphomet. This was especially true for Wicca, the largest religion to emerge from the Neopagan revival. Despite Baphomet's resemblance to the celebrated Horned God of the Witches, Wiccans generally didn't include Them in their rites. Wiccan covens arising in predominately Christian America and Britain often struggled to differentiate themselves from Satanists and thus avoided association with overtly Satanic symbols, including Lévi's Baphomet.

The result of LaVey's actions was that there were now two symbols associated with Baphomet: Lévi's esoteric Baphomet image and the Satanic Sigil of Baphomet. Christians saw no distinction between them, so both were promoted as symbols of Satan and evidence of devil worship, a public perception that persists in modern culture.

The Satanic Temple

Almost fifty years after the Church of Satan was established, another Satanic Baphomet appeared. The Satanic Temple (TST), a nontheistic religious organization, was founded in 2012 by Lucien Greaves and Malcolm Jarry. The logo for their new Satanic church is similar to the Sigil of Baphomet, with both symbols consisting of a goat's head in an upside-down pentagram within a circle. However, TST's goat head is a silhouette with more demonic features and is crowned with the flaming torch that symbolically identifies the head with Baphomet.

In contrast to the apolitical stance of the Church of Satan, TST is dedicated to political action, using its status as a recognized nonprofit religious organization as a platform to fight for equal representation in places where the separation of church and state is under threat. Their definition of Satan complements their emphasis on activism: "Satan is a symbol of the Eternal Rebel in opposition to arbitrary authority, forever defending personal sovereignty even in the face of insurmountable odds. Satan is an icon for the unbowed will of the unsilenced inquirer—the heretic who questions sacred laws and rejects all tyrannical impositions."[68] The Temple hails from the legacy of the Romantic Satanists, members of the nineteenth-century literary and political movement that redefined Satan as a heroic rebel who struggled against religious tyranny and political oppression.

In 2013, Greaves and Jarry sought to challenge the installation of a Ten Commandments monument on the grounds of the state capitol in Oklahoma, an obvious violation of the separation of church and state. They decided to create a Satanic monument, a statue of Baphomet, to be installed next to the Christian one, forc-

68. https://thesatanictemple.com/pages/faq.

ing Oklahoma to either honor the separation clause or remove the Ten Commandments from the capitol grounds.

The statue, titled "Baphomet with Children," was sculpted by Mark Porter and cast in bronze in 2014. Weighing more than 3000 pounds and standing over eight feet tall, the statue of Baphomet cost $100,000 to create, with $30,000 raised by members and supporters of a GoFundMe campaign. The design was based on Lévi's Baphomet icon but has no breasts, a concession to make the statue suitable for public display. Created "with 'respect for diversity and religious minorities' in mind," the black and white crescent moons from Lévi's image have been abstracted into black and white children, who stand on either side of the adoring Baphomet.[69]

The proposed installation of the Baphomet statue was canceled after the Oklahoma Supreme Court ruled in June 2015 that the Ten Commandments monument violated the state's ban on using public property to promote religion, and it was removed later that year. Undeterred, TST officially unveiled their Baphomet statue on July 25, 2015, at a ceremony in Detroit sensationalized by the mainstream media and demonized by superstitious Christians. Due to the controversy and protests by religious groups, the location of the unveiling ceremony was kept secret, and people who bought tickets to the event had to sign a contract selling their soul to the devil, a tactic used to deter Christian protesters. This event is commemorated on Unveiling Day, a TST holiday that celebrates "religious plurality and shedding archaic superstition."[70] The Baphomet statue is currently on display at TST's headquarters in Salem, Massachusetts, where people can sit on its lap and take photos of themselves to post on social media.

---

69. https://thesatanictemple.com/pages/holidays.

70. https://thesatanictemple.com/pages/holidays.

In a speech at a 2018 rally in Little Rock, Arkansas, Greaves defined Baphomet in the context of TST: "Good people of Arkansas and supporters of religious liberty, I present to you Baphomet: a symbol of pluralism, legal equality, tolerance, free inquiry, freedom of conscience, and reconciliation."[71] In other words, Baphomet symbolizes the general goals of TST as an organization. Baphomet also serves as the Temple's symbolic stand-in for Satan, which has generated a lot of publicity and controversy in Christian-majority America.

The link between TST's Baphomet and Satan was reinforced when a replica of their Baphomet statue appeared as the object of worship by Satanic witches in the 2018 Netflix series *Chilling Adventures of Sabrina*. TST sued for copyright infringement and for damaging the organization's reputation by portraying their statue as evil. In an interview with *Rolling Stone*, Greaves stated, "Given the show's utilization of the Baphomet statue to represent an evil cannibalistic cult, a perception falsely associated with Satanism even in modern times, TST would have denied its use to the show creators."[72] In the end, Netflix apologized, and the two parties agreed to an undisclosed settlement.

The political antics of TST attracted a lot of attention from the mainstream media, which in turn pushed Baphomet into the public spotlight. As a result, Baphomet became much more visible in popular culture, appearing on T-shirts, stickers, backpacks, and even bedspreads. Statues of Baphomet, once rare, are now common, as are cute cartoonish "baby Baphomet" plush toys. The Baphomet image has also been adopted by many people in the queer commu-

71. Joseph Laycock, *Speak of the Devil* (Oxford, 2020), 193.

72. Lilly Dancyger, "Satanic Temple Suing Netflix Over 'Sabrina' Statue Design," *Rolling Stone*, November 1, 2018. https://www.rollingstone.com/culture/culture-news/satanic-temple-suing-netflix-sabrina-statue-design-750868/.

nity in general and by transgender folks in particular, who identify with the deity's gender-fluid nature. Consequently, some conservative Christians have called out Baphomet as the Satanic god promoting the evil transgendered agenda. In any case, thanks to the Satanic Temple, Baphomet has become more visible than ever in the twenty-first century.

Baphomet has been linked with Satanism since the trial of the Templars. Catholics and con men fraudulently linked Baphomet to Satan to implicate the Masons in the nineteenth century. Lévi never thought Baphomet represented Satan, but then gave his image a goat's head adorned with a pentagram and a fiery torch—all symbols associated with Satan—to protect the occult secrets the image represented from the profane. Crowley, AKA the Great Beast of Thelema, who took on the name Baphomet as head of the O.T.O., was accused of being a satanist in the British press and is still considered to be a satanist by modern-day Christians.

Still, none of these folks would have ever guessed that Baphomet would be become a symbol of public, nontheistic Satanists like the TST. While the modern Baphomet-Satan connection initially discouraged Pagan involvement with the deity, as Paganism became more accepted and established at the end of the twentieth century, some Pagan practitioners started exploring their own conceptions of the esoteric Baphomet. We'll meet them in the second part of this book.

PART TWO

RITUAL

SOLVE
COAGULA

Chapter 5

Baphomet Reborn

In the late twentieth and early twenty-first centuries, Pagan practitioners from different spiritual paths started working with Baphomet and documenting their beliefs and experiences. We'll now examine four esoteric conceptions of Baphomet, focusing on their descriptions of the deity and how and why Pagan practitioners work with Them.

The first practical conception of the esoteric Baphomet arose in England sometime in the late 1970s. It's not exactly clear how Peter Carroll got involved with Baphomet, though coming from a ceremonial magic background, he was obviously influenced by Lévi and Crowley. Unlike his predecessors, Carroll's conception of Baphomet was far more logical and straightforward.

Evolving into Chaos

In Britain, the early Neopagan movement was dominated by Witchcraft and its offshoots, as well as by resurrected occult initiatory orders like the O.T.O. and the Golden Dawn. However, in the 1970s a new magical philosophy began to develop among a community of eclectic magicians drawn together by their interest in the works of English magician and artist Austin Osman Spare.

Spare's initial interest in occultism led him to join Crowley's A.·.A.·. in 1909, but Spare soon rejected Thelemic magic and developed his own unique magical system. What made Spare's system of magic special is that it worked without the rituals, equipment, and spiritual correspondences traditionally called for in modern occultism.

When Spare died, his work was preserved by his literary executor and friend, British occultist Kenneth Grant, who established the Typhonian O.T.O. in 1973 and claimed to be Crowley's successor as head of the O.T.O. Grant promoted the ideas of Spare both in his own writings, known as the Typhonian trilogies, and through the publication of some of Spare's work in *Images and Oracles of Austin Osman Spare* in 1975. Experimentation with Spare's ideas prompted this community of British magicians to create the modern magical system known as chaos magic.

Chaos magic can be difficult to define; like Spare's magical system, it focuses on getting results from magic without resorting to the complicated rituals and dogma found in traditional occult orders. Chaos magic uses belief as a tool to empower magic, and once results are obtained, one can use a different (or even contradictory) set of beliefs to energize the next working. Chaos magicians are encouraged to develop their own ritual and symbol systems, often accomplished by borrowing techniques and ideas from other spiritual or cultural traditions. Chaos magicians are also compelled to question the nature and perception of objective truth, a philosophy summarized in the Nihilist saying, "Nothing is true, everything is permitted."

The popularity of chaos magic in the late 1970s led to the formation of the Illuminates of Thanateros (IOT), a nonhierarchical magical order dedicated to the practice and exploration of chaos magic. In 1987, the commercial publication of *Liber Null & Psy-*

chonaut by Peter Carroll, one of the founders of chaos magic and the IOT, exposed this modern system to a much wider audience. Originally published as two separate books, *Liber Null* is a syllabus of the magical techniques and philosophy practiced by individuals in the IOT; *Psychonaut* is a series of related essays on chaos magic, "source material and a work of reference for those who seek to perform group magic or to work as shamanic priests to the community."[73] *Liber Null & Psychonaut* was the first book on the subject to be picked up by a major occult publisher, and it soon became the quintessential book on chaos magic. It is also the book that brought the esoteric Baphomet into the modern era.

The Earthly Deity of Chaos

Carroll defines chaos as "the animating force of the entire vast universe:"

> It is the inexpressible pregnant void from which manifest existence, order, and form arise. Being omnipresent and nondualistic, it is virtually imperceptible, inconceivable, and impossible to visualize. Almost any attempt to say anything about it would be a denial of its other qualities and so a lie.[74]

This infinite force is completely incomprehensible to the human mind, and thus it is impossible for us to understand or manipulate it. The key to working with chaos is to narrow our focus from the universal down to the planetary level:

> There is a part of chaos which is of more direct relevance to the magician. This is the spirit of the life energy of

73. Peter Carroll, *Liber Null & Psychonaut* (Samuel Weiser, 1987), 93.
74. Carroll, *Liber Null & Psychonaut*, 139.

> our planet. All living beings have some extra quality in them which separates them from inorganic matter. The ancient shamans mainly sought to represent this force by the Horned God. In more modern times, this force has reasserted itself in our awareness under the symbol of Baphomet.[75]

As the spirit of the life energy of the planet, Baphomet has been around as long as life has existed upon the planet, making Them a very ancient god indeed. Carroll connects Baphomet with the "animating spirit of living beings," an entity known to prehistoric humanity as the Horned God:

> It was a force without morality, and it could not be bargained with nor placated. However, by careful observation, mediation, and training, it was possible to give oneself and one's tribe a psychic edge in a hostile environment by its appreciation.
>
> These early psychic abilities, coupled with a high intelligence, rapidly made the puny humans into the planet's most successful species. The force that made this possible was universally symbolized as the Horned God. Horned because it conferred certain powers over animals and a horned human because it represented something extra which humans could acquire. The double horns symbolize the bipolar nature of a force which was both good and evil, light and dark, beautiful and terrible. Furthermore, the horned-god image gives an impression of the awesome and fearful nature of this type of power.[76]

75. Carroll, *Liber Null & Psychonaut*, 140.
76. Carroll, *Liber Null & Psychonaut*, 138.

As the Horned God, Baphomet helped prehistoric humanity survive and flourish, initiating the process of human evolution. In this way, Baphomet is at least partially responsible for the success of the human race.

Aeons of the Horned God

To document our relationship with the Horned God, Carroll divides human history into five Aeons based on our spiritual and intellectual progress.

In the Shamanistic Aeon, prehistoric humanity recognized that all living things were animated by a spiritual force often depicted as a Horned God. Our appreciation and understanding of the nature of the Horned God was one of the things that gave humans an edge in the struggle to survive in the ancient world.

When humanity developed agriculture and started to settle down in the Pagan Aeon, we started to lose touch with this force of nature. Polytheism and pantheism emerged, as aspects of the Horned God were personified as deities.

In the Monotheistic Aeon, church and state united under an idealized male god who offered divine sanction for secular authority and proscribed religious morality to shape and control citizens. The gods of the previous Aeon became devils, and the Horned God reappeared as the anti-god associated with witches and sorcerers.

In the Atheistic Aeon, which many cultures on Earth are currently passing through, God becomes human, but humanity's fixation with physical technology and science causes it to lose its connection to the spiritual world, and the Horned God becomes the hidden god.

We are now on the cusp of the Chaoist Aeon, which Carroll speculates will lead to a confluence of science and magic that will change the way we understand and employ both concepts—much like chaos magic. In this Aeon, the previously hidden Horned One reveals itself as Baphomet.

To summarize, humanity develops a strong and intimate connection with the Horned One in the Shamanistic Aeon, but in each subsequent Aeon, our connection with the Horned One weakens. However, recent changes in the way we understand the relationship between science and magic have brought the Horned One back into human consciousness. Our relationship with the Horned One dissolved over time, but presently it is coagulating in the form of Baphomet.

Reimagining the Icon

Carroll's discussion also offers some innovative ideas regarding the traditional iconography associated with Baphomet:

> No image can fully represent the totality of what this force is, but it is conventionally shown as a hermaphrodite god-goddess in the form of a horned human that includes various mammalian and reptilian characteristics. It should also resume protozoan, insectivorous, and floral symbolism, for it is the animating spirit of everything from a bacterium to a tiger. If we succeed in creating machine consciousness, it will have to include mechanical elements as well.[77]

The ideal Baphomet image would include not only all forms of life but also the emblems of death:

> Life and death are a single phenomenon through which the life force continually reincarnates. A denial of death is

77. Carroll, *Liber Null & Psychonaut,* 140–41.

> also a denial of life. The cellular mechanisms which allow life also make death inevitable, essential, and desirable.[78]

Finally, the sexual elements of Baphomet are also important: "The sexual aspects of the god-goddess Baphomet are always emphasized, for sex creates life, and sexuality is a measure of the life force or vitality, no matter how it is expressed."[79] Death and sex are characterized in chaos magic as representative of the destructive and creative forces of the universe, the forces used in all magical workings. This relationship is expressed in the term *Thanateros*, a combination of the names Thanatos, the Greek god of death, and Eros, the Greek god of erotic love.

Carroll also suggests that the combination of human, goat, and serpent characteristics found in the traditional Baphomet image reflect the evolutionary structure of the human brain. He refers to triune brain theory, which postulates that the human brain is comprised of a reptile brain (governing the basic survival instincts we share with reptiles) covered by a mammal brain (governing lower brain functions), which is in turn covered by a human brain (responsible for higher brain functions). In other words, "the human has an ape, a wolf, and a crocodile living inside its skull."[80]

He then indicates that the older reptile and mammal brains can be accessed and activated to empower magical work:

> Society and religions have been concerned with keeping the dragon and the wolf permanently suppressed, except at such times as it suited them to make war. For the magician, these atavistic forces are a source of personal power. Thus Baphomet, the magicians' god, is frequently shown

78. Carroll, *Liber Null & Psychonaut*, 141.
79. Carroll, *Liber Null & Psychonaut*, 141.
80. Carroll, *Liber Null & Psychonaut*, 142.

in composite human-mammal-serpent form, as are many shamanic gods.[81]

The Mass of Baphomet

The only group ritual script presented in *Psychonaut* is the Mass of Chaos B, with the B signifying Baphomet. In this ritual, the participants invoke Baphomet into a priest or priestess, then use the powerful energy of the deity to accomplish the ritual's specific purpose, be it invocation, evocation, divination, enchantment, or consecration. It is not a complicated ritual, and there is a lot of room for the participants to customize the ritual as desired.

The Star of Chaos (Chaostar)

After the participants set up the temple and mentally prepare themselves for ritual work, the officiant states the intent of the ritual. They then lead the group in the Invocation of Chaos by drawing an eight-pointed Star of Chaos, the primary symbol of chaos magic, above the circle. The other participants assist the officiant by visualizing and energizing the Star of Chaos while the officiant recites the "barbarous incantation" of Chaos; here is a rough translation:

I reign over you, saith the Dragon Eagle of the Primal Chaos
I am the First, the Highest that live in the First Aethyr

81. Carroll, *Liber Null & Psychonaut*, 143.

I am the Terror of the Earth, the Horns of Death
Pouring down the Fires of Life on the Earth[82]

The Invocation of Baphomet begins with the officiant taking on physical aspects of Baphomet, such donning a horned headdress or bearing one's breasts, and visualizing themselves in the form of the god Baphomet. The officiant invokes and cycles the power of the life-force within themselves. The other participants assist by invoking Baphomet into the officiant and projecting the energy of the life-force into their own manifestations.

At the climax of the ritual, the officiant completes the invocation with an oration identifying themselves with Baphomet, an invocation known as the aeonic litany:

In the first aeon, I was the Great Spirit.
In the second aeon, Men knew me as the Horned God,
Pangenitor Panphage.
In the third aeon, I was the Dark One, the Devil.
In the fourth aeon, Men know me not, for I am the Hidden One.
In this new aeon, I appear before you as Baphomet.
The God before all gods who shall endure to the end of the Earth.[83]

The officiant, acting as Baphomet, takes any material basis that was used as a focus of the rite (such as food or drink for a eucharist, a sigil for an evocation or enchantment, etc.) and consecrates it "by whatever means the god wills, perhaps by speech, by gesture, or by some unexpected means."[84] To complete the ritual, this material basis is presented to the group while the officiant

82. Carroll, *Liber Null & Psychonaut*, 112–13.
83. Carroll, *Liber Null & Psychonaut*, 113.
84. Carroll, *Liber Null & Psychonaut*, 114.

and participants state, "This is my will." The material basis is then consumed, destroyed, or hidden according to the purpose of the ritual, and Baphomet is banished or exorcised from the officiant.

The Mass of Chaos B is the closest thing the IOT has to an official ritual; it was performed at the opening and closing of their annual meetings. Furthermore, the nature of the ritual has changed over the years:

> For many years The Mass of Chaos B was often attended by incidents of spilled wine and chaotic rage. As the IOT matured, the Mass altered slightly; an atmosphere of harmonious diversity provided Baphomet with a less fearful welcome, and joyous celebration became the general default setting.[85]

The Eight Qualities

In 2014, Carroll published his most recent work, *Epoch*, which consists of two parts: a book titled *The Esotericon* and a 52-card deck called the *Portals of Chaos*. *The Esotericon* is Carroll's magnum opus; it presents a new system of magic synthesized from elements of modern occultism and concepts of chaos magick found in Carroll's previous works. The central glyph of the system is called the Choabala, considered to be the Qabala of the Chaoist Aeon.

The Chaobala consists of three connected realms: the Five Elements, the Octaris Mindstar of Planetary Magic, and the Elder Gods of Stellar Magic. Each circular realm is made up of spheres containing symbols representative of the entities and deities within the realm. For example, the realm of the Five Elements consists of five spheres marked with Hindu Tattva symbols for the elements;

85. Nikki Wyrd and Julian Vayne, *The Book of Baphomet* (Mandrake, 2012), 142.

they are arranged and connected to form an upright pentagram, with the element of Aethyr (spirit) at the pentagram's top.

The Chaobala from Carroll's *Esotericon*

The realms of the Five Elements and the Octaris Mindstar are connected by a single sphere that serves as the gatekeeper between them: the sphere of Baphomet. Carroll devotes a small section of his book to Baphomet, where he briefly discusses Lévi's life and ideas, then identifies the "seven obvious qualities" of Lévi's image:

DUALISTIC: It looks both light and dark, a sort of God-Devil.

ANDROGYNOUS: It includes both male and female features.

LUCIFERIC: It carries a torch, as a bringer of illumination and forbidden wisdom.

THERIOMORPHIC: It looks half human, half animal, Pan like, Pagan, incorporating the 'lower selfs' as well as the 'higher'. It includes symbols of reptilian, avian, and mammalian life, and it sits on a cube for the element earth, placed upon a sphere for the world.

SEXUALIZED: It has breasts and a symbolic penis, and a Goat-like horny / satanic appearance.

MAGICAL: It bears a Caduceus wand and makes magical gestures, and it bears magical symbols as it sits beneath the waxing and waning moons. Its arms bear the alchemical ciphers of Solve and Coagula, and its fingers show the mysterious number 23, two points upward, three down for the hidden averse pentagram perhaps, to balance the upright one on its brow.

SHAMANIC: It looks like the Horned Gods of many shamanic traditions and early pagan religions, which became the Devils of the monotheistic religions.[86]

Carroll then identifies an eighth quality added by modern magicians—Baphomet is GAIANISTIC:

They have added GAIA, a sense of the sacredness of the Biosphere and Ecology, Life on Earth. The realisation

---

86. Peter Carroll, *Epoch: The Esotericon & Portals of Chaos* (Arcanorum College, 2014), 39.

> that humans do not exist separate from nature but rather that they exist as large brained animals still largely driven by their reptilian and mammalian circuits but just clever enough to realise their own mortality, their own promethean and magical potential, and their utter dependency on evolution, sex and death, their own planet, and all other life upon it, which leads to the realisation that this planet and everything on it constitutes a vast Panpsychic organism, a god form of the planet of which we now form a part, the first god that humans consciously identified as 'the great spirit', who shall endure till the end of the world, with or without us, changing its forms as it evolves.[87]

The Greek goddess Gaia is one of the more common names of the earth goddess invoked by many Neopagan faiths, particularly Wicca. The name is also linked with the Gaia hypothesis formulated by English scientist James Lovelock, which proposes that the biosphere functions like a living organism, its living and nonliving elements working together to maintain a self-regulating system that supports life.

Carroll's Panpsychic organism unites spirituality with science. Panpsychism is the belief that all matter (living and non-living) possesses some element of consciousness; Gaia is the personification of the whole planet (living and nonliving) as a conscious entity. If all matter possesses an element of consciousness, then it's possible that the biosphere might also be conscious, functioning as a living organism as proposed by the Gaia hypothesis. Of course, Carroll's Panpsychic organism is none other than Baphomet.

---

87. Carroll, *Epoch*, 40. Some of the modern magicians of which he speaks are featured in the next chapter.

A Twenty-First-Century Icon

Carroll's Baphomet section also includes a full-color illustration of the deity created by artist Matt Kaybryn in collaboration with Carroll, who gives us a description of the image in *The Esotericon*:

> Our image shows a theriomorphic figure standing on the curve of the planet Earth straddling a continent or two. It has goat legs to symbolize the mammalian kingdom, and a furred groin which leaves gender unspecified, the scales of the fish and reptile kingdoms show on its belly, it has human arms and a bare torso with female breasts, an androgynous face with a chaostar for multiple possibilities on its brow beneath its horns. It has wings for aspiration and it carries a wand in the shape of a phallus with a DNA spiral around it in one hand and a torch in the other. At its feet lie the skulls of its own ancestors and descendants, stretching off into the distance, and amongst them other terrestrial creatures dance and plants grow.[88]

Carroll has preserved many of the elements of Lévi's Baphomet image and added a few of his own. The upright pentagram on the forehead of Lévi's image has been replaced by a Chaostar representing "multiple possibilities." Carroll's Baphomet wields Lévi's phallic wand (the caduceus) and the torch of illumination. Lévi's cubic throne is gone and Baphomet stands directly upon the earth. Most significantly, the prominent goat's head that many have linked with satanism has been replaced by an androgynous human head.

The new Baphomet also includes additional symbolism Carroll proposed more than twenty-five years ago in *Liber Null &*

---

88. Carroll, *Epoch*, 40.

Psychonaut.[89] Baphomet's hair consists of leafy vines that cascade from Their head and wrap around Their right leg, and plants flourish where They stand upon the earth. Insects fly in the air around Baphomet, and some of the dancing "terrestrial creatures" (which are a little difficult to see in the image) could be protozoa and bacteria. Human, mammal, reptile, protozoan, insect, floral, bacterium—it's all in there! Plus the skulls are symbols of death. which complement the life-giving phallic wand.

At the end of the Baphomet section, Carroll urges us to invoke Baphomet "to unlock the riches within" and "to commune with the terrestrial riches all around" and suggests using the Mass of Chaos B to accomplish these tasks.[90]

While Aleister Crowley may have initiated the process of the deification of Baphomet, Carroll completed the process. Unlike Crowley, Carroll clearly defined the nature of Baphomet and revealed Their significance to the modern magician. Carroll was also the first magician to present a ritual solely dedicated to invoking and working with Baphomet. Finally, Carroll was the first magician to reestablish the esoteric Baphomet in modern occultism after Baphomet became associated with the Church of Satan in the 1970s.

In *The Esotericon*, Carroll establishes Baphomet as the ruler of the realm of the five elements. He identifies Baphomet with the Earth's biosphere, realizing Them as a "vast Panpsychic organism" that connects everything on the planet. Finally, Carroll and Kaybryn present a new icon of Baphomet for the twenty-first century that clearly reflects Their connection to the earth.

---

89. See "The Eight Qualities," pages 104–106.

90. Carroll, *Epoch*, 40.

Chapter 6

A Greener Baphomet

Twenty-five years after *Liber Null & Psychonaut* established Baphomet as a deity of chaos magic, chaos magicians Nikki Wyrd and Julian Vayne published *The Book of Baphomet* (2012), one of the first books dedicated to the esoteric Baphomet. Peter Carroll established Baphomet as an esoteric deity for the modern era; *The Book of Baphomet* is a deeper exploration of this deity and its evolution within chaos magic, and it presents some fascinating insights into how to understand and work with the esoteric Baphomet.

Like many books in the chaos magic genre, *The Book of Baphomet* is a collection of essays woven together into a semi-linear whole around a primary theme; in this case, the theme is the history, meaning, and magic of Baphomet. The book can be divided into three parts: the main body of the book that discusses Baphomet, an account of the creation and performance of the authors' Circle of Baphomet ritual, and a six-week program of exercises that prepare you to perform your own invocation of Baphomet.

The Natural Connection

The Baphomet Wyrd and Vayne describe has a more direct connection with nature than that presented by Carroll. Carroll's Horned God, "the spirit of the life energy of the planet," comes across as a force within nature, but to the authors of *The Book of Baphomet*, Baphomet *is* nature. The authors' conception of Baphomet includes not only the life-force of the planet but also the non-living elements that support life, such as the rocks, the air, and even the inorganic compounds essential to life. Their animistic conception of the biosphere expanded the size and scope of Baphomet a few years before Carroll labeled Baphomet as a Panpsychic organism.

Furthermore, the authors not only connect Baphomet with nature but also with Baphomet *through* nature. Most accounts of individual and group Baphomet workings described in *The Book of Baphomet* happen in nature, outside of civilization. In many ways their Baphomet is similar to the Goddess of Wicca and Witchcraft, which is not surprising considering both are deifications of nature.

Finally, Wyrd and Vayne acknowledge the damage that humans have done to the natural world and seek ways to change humanity's relationship with the earth:

> Baphomet is first and foremost the deity of the life force of earth. Humanity is waking up to our role and responsibility in terms of that life force. In the twinkling of a geological eye we have made huge impacts on the planet and excelled in a dizzying propagation of technology. We have so deeply influenced the earth that the geological era in which we live is known as the Anthropocene. We have generated a vast number of meta-modules of awareness, many machines and skills. If we are that life force becoming self-aware then our awareness first

> sees that until now most of us were sleeping. Worse, on awakening we discover that we've been sleep walking, are injured, and that we've made one hell of a mess in the temple. We awake only to discover that we've massively changed the climate, that our current culture is poised on the brink of disaster. We've emerged from the deep sleep of the last 10,000 years and woken to the nightmare of resource depletion, gargantuan weapons, huge social inequality and immanent ecological meltdown. The next stage is to wake fully. To realise Baphomet in all hir forms, to arise from the trance.[91]

The impending disaster is reflected in the turbulent transition between the current Atheistic Aeon and the emerging Chaoist Aeon. In Carroll's Aeonic model, our connection with the Horned God, our spiritual connection with Nature, weakens with each successive Aeon, and now there is a price to pay. Our infatuation with science in the Atheistic Aeon has caused us to lose our connection with the spiritual world and Baphomet, allowing the damage to nature to accelerate. The authors seek to raise awareness of this process of natural destruction and ultimately arrest it until the unfolding Chaoist Aeon reconnects us with Nature and Baphomet and we develop a more harmonious relationship with the earth. They also stress that we have to change our ways soon, before we destroy the world and ourselves along with it: "There is no alternative to this awakening except extinction."[92] Wake up or die, humans.

Wyrd and Vayne also pursue a related line of investigation: how did humanity get so out of sync with the natural world? *The*

---

91. Wyrd and Vayne, *The Book of Baphomet*, 146–47.
92. Wyrd and Vayne, *The Book of Baphomet*, 38.

Book of Baphomet not only examines the history and magic of Baphomet but also discusses the history of how we lost our connection to nature:

> Historically, we can point a finger at The Enlightenment, the dawn of scientific thinking. Transport ourselves back to that time and place; superstitious preachings from Mother Church abound, bizarre folk customs dictating society's conduct. A need for a less passionate, more verifiable mode of decision making needs to arise. Enter Science, with The Royal Society acting as a common ground for people from all religions, classes, and backgrounds, to meet and discuss a topic with a blank page, starting from observation of reality instead of ancient writings.
>
> They needed to turn their backs on visions and voices, look at numbered certainties amidst a sea of ritualised stagnant ceremonies. Without this move our world would not have achieved a realistic view of How Things Work. However... this focus on the rational to the exclusion of all else has left us damaged. Our task now centres on ways of revaluing the arational, as a qualitatively essential perspective. Restricting value to numbered quantities results in money choices ruling our lives to the cost of understanding other values, some which mean more to us, as animals.[93]

Connecting with Nature in general and Baphomet in particular is the key to restoring the balance between the rational and the irrational, the measurable (science) and the immeasurable

93. Wyrd and Vayne, *The Book of Baphomet*, 74–75.

(nature). The authors also encourage us to understand that we are a part of nature, not separate from it:

> How many ordinary folk would identify themselves as natural? I fear that most of us cannot help but to define man-made and natural as entirely separate categories; this Us and Them approach lies at the root of so many societal ills, we must invest considerable endeavour towards removing this distinction.... Not only are we natural, we are now a true Force of Nature, greater than the giants of old, destroying mountains, moving rivers, altering the levels of the oceans, changing the air we breathe.[94]

Working with Baphomet is one way to bridge this conceptual gap, which is the focus of the last two sections of Wyrd and Vayne's book. It can be divided into three parts: the main body that discusses Baphomet, an account of the creation and performance of the authors' Circle of Baphomet ritual, and a six-week program of exercises that prepare the reader to perform their own invocation of Baphomet. Finally, to continue their exploration of Baphomet and chaos magic, the authors have established *The Blog of Baphomet*, "a magickal dialogue between nature and culture."[95]

The Circle of Baphomet Ritual

In the process of writing their book, the authors strove to understand the nature of the modern Baphomet. Like Carroll, Wyrd and Vayne believed Lévi's original image of the deity was limited and incomplete. "The first intention was to attempt a new conceptualization of Baphomet... a new god, a god of the Aeon that was

94. Wyrd and Vayne, *The Book of Baphomet*, 88.
95. https://theblogofbaphomet.com.

incoming."[96] Their investigations and experiences revealed a deity that is omnipresent in nature, connected to and connecting with everything on the planet, possibly even the universe as well.

Their next impulse was to write a ritual to share their conception of the deity with other magicians. Wyrd and Vayne had primarily used sex magick to attain their vision of Baphomet, but that method was not appropriate for group magical workings. By chance they happened upon the perfect sacrament for their new ritual: DMT.[97]

One key component of chaos magic is the use of altered states of consciousness to bypass the censor of the conscious mind, the ego that interferes with magical work. There are a number of methods of achieving altered states of consciousness, including dancing, drumming, chanting, fasting, sensory deprivation, sexual arousal, pain, and many others. One of the more popular methods is the use of mind-altering drugs.

In addition to their passion for chaos magic, Wyrd and Vayne are also both active in the movement promoting the experimentation and legalization of entheogens. Entheogens (Latin: "god within") are psychoactive substances that produce dramatic altered states of consciousness that can be used in religious or spiritual contexts. The authors report that they can "produce a fresh approach to the world," by "allowing a reset of established patterns."[98] Entheogens also "allow us to perceive the deep structures of the universe."[99]

---

96. Wyrd and Vayne, *The Book of Baphomet*, 179.
97. Specifically, they used 5-MeO-DMT, which produces significantly different effects than the more common N, N-DMT.
98. Wyrd and Vayne, *The Book of Baphomet*, 170.
99. Wyrd and Vayne, *The Book of Baphomet*, 163.

DMT (dimethyltryptamine), a powerful hallucinogen found in the venom of the Sonoran desert toad (and also in high concentrations in certain plants), had the effect they were looking for in their ritual to connect people with the life force of the earth. Vayne's first experience with DMT convinced him that they had found the right catalyst for connecting with Baphomet:

> Very little visual content, instead this was the sense and the definitely physical sensation of plunging into another world. Down the toad hole I travelled. My hands were pressed into the floor, my body curled up into a foetal position. Deeper and deeper into the earth, into the heart of things and at the same time the sense of expanding, being blown up, as large as the whole of the universe. I was in the core of reality, at the limitless extension of all that changes—I was one with Baphomet.[100]

Keep in mind that both Wyrd and Vayne have extensive knowledge and experience with entheogens. They have lectured at conferences on entheogens, conferred with scientists and other researchers, and spoken with many people about their experiences with these drugs. They have also experimented with entheogens in many different spiritual contexts and shared their own research and experiences with others in books and journals. Especially in group rituals, using entheogens is *not* recommended without extensive prior research on how to safely employ these substances to produce alternative states of consciousness. You have been warned.

The Circle of Baphomet ritual was performed a couple of times in the process of development, first with only a chosen few, later with more people as more elements were added and the process

---

100. Wyrd and Vayne, *The Book of Baphomet*, 181.

refined. The authors do not provide a ritual script; here's a basic outline of the final ritual described in the book:

1. People walk to the ritual site to the beat of a slow drum and form a circle.
2. They engage in Horns of Baphomet yoga (described in their book).
3. They slowly spiral into the center of the circle while being made aware that they are travelling the billions of years that life evolved from single-cell organisms into the complex forms of life around us.
4. They partake of the four elements: scented herbs for air, honey for fire, water, and rich soil for earth.
5. Those wishing to partake of DMT remain in the center of the circle, while the others withdraw to chant, drum, and offer support.
6. Those in the center smoke DMT and experience visions.
7. When everyone has returned to regular consciousness, the ritual closes with the "Mithraic salute of fellowship": shaking hands.[101]

At the end of this section, the authors included participants' descriptions of what they experienced after smoking the DMT. Needless to say, these are all very bizarre and intense, but most participants felt that they had connected with Baphomet. The authors believe that the Circle of Baphomet ritual achieved its desired result:

> Chaos magicians to the last, this process has a definite intent, a definable result; namely that the people in the rite, and all those they touch would begin to feel their

101. See Wyrd and Vayne, *The Book of Baphomet*, 174–94.

> lived connection to the earth. Our aim was (and is) that rather than just thinking about, or intellectually knowing our relationship in the biosphere, it should be felt, and felt intensely. That feeling should contribute to our sustainable unfolding as a species. Feeling ourselves rooted deep within the earth, we reach for the stars.[102]

Baphomet Through the Spheres

Entheogens aren't the only way to connect with Baphomet. At the end of their book, Wyrd and Vayne provide a series of practical exercises that lead to an invocation of Baphomet. With some preparation and work, these exercises allow the individual to connect with the life force of the planet on their own, no entheogens required.

The inspiration for this working is the Gnostic Chaosphere Ritual (GCR), a solo banishing and centering ritual created by Peter Carroll with help from Nikki Wyrd. The GCR builds on the Gnostic Pentagram Ritual from Carroll's second book, *Liber Kaos*, linking the five vowels of the English alphabet used in the original ritual with the five Spheres of Chaos. Representing layers of reality and perspectives of the universe, the Spheres of Chaos are the Panpsychosphere, the world of possibilities and magic; the Noosphere, the world of thoughts and ideas; the Anthrosphere, the world of humanity; the Biosphere, the world of life; and the Geosphere, the world of the "inanimate" planet. Note that these spheres do not represent any kind of hierarchical arrangement; they are perspectives and nothing more.

102. Wyrd and Vayne, *The Book of Baphomet*, 183.

Table 1
Correspondences of the Gnostic Chaosphere Ritual[103]

Sphere	Vowel	Symbol	Chakra
Panpsychosphere	I	Chaos star	Brow
Noosphere	E	Tellus	Throat
Anthrosphere	A	Upright pentagram	Heart
Biosphere	O	Baphometic pentagram	Solar plexus
Geosphere	U	Earth symbol	Perineum

The Baphomet Through the Spheres working is a five-week exploration of Baphomet in each of the Spheres of Chaos. Wyrd explains the process: "The spheres of the GCR indicated to me a set of perspectives from which to approach this deity of our world, this larger-than-life character, bigger than the sum of the parts; yet by starting from the parts one can make an attempt at grokking the whole."[104] Each week focuses on Baphomet in one of the five Spheres, starting with the Geosphere and ending with the Panpsychosphere. Exercises are given to help you connect to Baphomet in each Sphere. After completing this exploration, the challenge of the sixth week is to integrate the things you have learned by constructing a full invocation of Baphomet and performing it.

103. Wyrd and Vayne, *The Book of Baphomet*, 201–02.
104. Wyrd and Vayne, *The Book of Baphomet*, 204.

The Craft of Baphomet

A couple of years after *The Book of Baphomet* came out, Vayne and another IOT member, Steve Dee, published another account of magical work involving Baphomet titled *Chaos Craft*. Chaos Craft is a magical paradigm that brings together chaos magic and Wicca by combining the eight celebrations of the Wiccan Wheel of the Year with the eight colors of magic discussed by Carroll in *Liber Kaos* (see table 2).

Table 2
The Wheel of the Year from *Chaos Craft*[105]

Season	Color	Direction	Magic
Imbolc	Green	Northeast	Love and sacrifice, parenthood, the promise of spring
Spring Equinox	Orange	East	The incoming power of the year
Beltane	Purple	Southeast	Sex
Midsummer	Yellow	South	The self, the waking consciousness
Lammas	Red	Southwest	Agriculture, war, John Barleycorn must die

105. Julian Vayne and Steve Dee, *Chaos Craft: The Wheel of the Year in Eight Colours* (The Universe Machine, 2016), 22.

Table 2 (Continued)
The Wheel of the Year from *Chaos Craft*[106]

Season	Color	Direction	Magic
Autumn Equinox	Blue	West	Wealth, reflecting on what we have gathered in the year
Samhain	Black	Northwest	Death
Yule	Octarine	North	The sun at midnight, the paradox and play of festival, the birth of the God Son

In this paradigm, the role of the Goddess is filled by Baphomet, the patron deity of Chaos Craft, as explained by Steve Dee:

> In *The Book of Baphomet*, Nikki and Julian put forward the idea that part of Baphomet's suitability as a god of our age is primarily due to hir being a glyph or image in search of a mythology. This is part of hir appeal as a deity for those of us who choose to work with hir—we sort through the scattered fragments of backstory trying to make sense of our experience viewed through the lenses of Lévi's infamous depiction and our own ritual experimentation. This sense of mythic fluidity and shape-

106. Julian Vayne and Steve Dee, *Chaos Craft: The Wheel of the Year in Eight Colours* (The Universe Machine, 2016), 22.

> shifting is arguably why ze proves to be such a vital patron for those of us undertaking magickal exploration.[107]

The rituals used to celebrate the wheel of the year are profoundly idiosyncratic, with individual participants presenting their own rituals or other contributions as elements of a larger working, with a hybrid theme based on the color of magic and the festival of the year. However, one of the standard group rituals presented in Chaos Craft, the Gates of Baphomet ritual, works directly with Baphomet in a strangely familiar way.

The Gates of Baphomet Ritual

The Gates of Baphomet ritual is a variation of the Mass of Chaos B reworked to fit into the Chaos Craft paradigm. The structure of the two rituals is essentially the same: the priest and participants invoke Baphomet into a person, and the person possessed by Baphomet performs a magical act (in this case, consecrates a chalice); then the priest exorcises Baphomet from the person and the chalice with the sacrament of Baphomet is shared with all present. What's interesting about the Gates of Baphomet ritual is how different techniques are used to achieve the same result.

The ritual requires a priest, a vessel, and five gatekeepers; each gatekeeper is assigned one of the Spheres of Chaos. The gatekeepers stand equidistant in a circle, with the priest and vessel in the center. The ritual begins with each gatekeeper declaring the name of their Sphere of Chaos, then vibrating the appropriate vowel sound. As this is done, the priest, using a Baphomet mudra, touches the part of the body of the vessel where the Sphere is located according to the GCR, and the two repeat the vowel

107. Vayne and Dee, *Chaos Craft*, 41–42.

sound. This part of the ritual consecrates the circle and installs Baphomet energy within the vessel.

Next the vessel kneels in front of the priest, who holds the vessel's head while intoning the invocation:

> *Baphomet! I am present here, DJ of the biosphere! Ramify! Join together! Open our eyes! Do life, do death, do sex with us!*[108]

When Baphomet has filled the vessel, they proclaim the Charge of Baphomet:

> *Hear now the Word of Madness and Mystery!*
> *I am movement and chaos, and I am the stillness inside of you.*
> *Self-born, untaught, motherless, unshakable.*
> *Giving place to no name, many-named, dwelling in fire.*
> *I am the secret Serpent coiled about to spring and in my coiling there is joy.*
> *I have made a hollow skin, from the heart of the holy tree,*
> *I compassed the earth therein, and rise from the depths of the Sea.*
> *I who am the beauty of the green earth, and the white moon among the stars, the soul of nature, that gives life to the universe.*
> *I who am the taste of honey and the swirl of flies,*
> *I the dragon wing of night overspreading the earth.*
> *I come with trumpets sounding shrill. Over the hill!*
> *I come with drums low muttering. From the spring!*
> *I come with flute and come with pipe! Am I not ripe?*

108. Vayne and Dee, *Chaos Craft*, 150–51. The English translation of the "barbaric" language is given.

I who am a Spear that roars for blood, and a Salmon in a pool,
a Lure from Paradise, and a Hill where poets walk.
I am that one-pointed awareness, radiating out in all directions.
From Me all things proceed, and unto Me all things must return.
I call to your soul; arise and come unto me!
For I am the voice of the song of life,
I am (insert names of living things, other inspired utterances ...)
I am Baphomet![109]

The vessel projects Baphomet energy into the chalice and offers it to the priest, who drinks. The priest draws a chaostar to banish Baphomet from the vessel, then offers the chalice to the vessel, who drinks from it and then passes it on to another participant until all have partaken.

Closing the Circle

There is a final ritual at the end of *Chaos Craft* worth mentioning, titled "Acknowledging our Selves as Baphomet":

> At the end of many of the Chaos Craft rituals the members of the coven sit together, cross-legged in a circle. We begin by holding hands (because that's always nice) and take three breaths together. (For the sky above us, for the earth beneath us, and for the water surrounding our island of Britain. This technique is borrowed from

109. Vayne and Dee, *Chaos Craft*, 151–52. Note: The Charge has been reformatted to promote clarity.

modern Druidry.) Participants then raise their right hand toward the sky, their left hand pointing towards the ground.

We say together:

From the Heights of the Heavens ... (looking up, right)

To the Depths of the Earth ... (looking down, left)

Folding hands together over our own chest, say:

We are one Heart.

Reaching out to either side to touch the hearts of those sitting beside us, say:

Connected.[110]

This closing ritual acknowledges the connection between Baphomet, the biosphere, and the ritualists, reminding everyonc about this connection before they depart.

The Baphomet of Wyrd, Vayne, and Dee is synonymous with Nature, an animistic conception of the deity for the emerging Chaoist Aeon. The authors explore this natural conception of Baphomet and interact with Them though ritual work in natural settings. Wyrd and Vayne provide their readers with solo rituals that allow magicians to make their own natural connection with Baphomet.

Wyrd and Vayne were the first to link Baphomet with the threat that climate change poses to our biosphere. They acknowl-

110. Vayne and Dee, *Chaos Craft*, 257.

edge that an important part of working with Baphomet is learning to change our destructive relationship with the planet, in part by reconnecting with Nature. Finally, they warn us that we must wake up and take responsibility for our actions before we destroy ourselves and the planet.

SOLVE

Chapter 7

A Modern Sabbat

By the end of the twentieth century, Wicca and other Pagan religions had become more established and accepted within society, giving Pagans more room to explore the darker sides of spirituality. In the first decade of the new millennium, a group of Australian witches ran a festival built around rituals exploring and confronting these darker aspects of life—and Baphomet was at the center of it all.

Creating Euphoria

There was trouble at the 1999 Pagan Summer Gathering. The annual event drew Pagan practitioners from all over Australia to a site outside Canberra to participate in ritual work, educational workshops, and community building. That year, one coven from Victoria performed a ritual called the Baphomet Rite. The rite's purpose, laid out in the ritual proposal submitted to the festival organizers, was read to attendees gathered before the commencement of the ritual. The proposal, crafted by Hawthorn, began with the following:

> The general gist of this statement was that the BAPHOMET rite was a paganised re-creation of the Witches Sabbat which was intended to invoke archetypal Witch energies, challenge conventional social interpretations of these energies, and liberate the ecstatic nature of the participants. The statement also warned that the rite contained nudity, sexual references and adult themes.[111]

This Baphomet Rite turned proposal out to be so controversial that some people tried to disrupt the ritual by singing nursery rhymes and the theme of the film *The Wizard of Oz*, "We're Off to See the Wizard," which only encouraged the ritualists and drummers to turn up the volume. The increased volume drove off the protesters, and the rite commenced without a hitch.

The day after the Baphomet Rite, the ritualists involved were called into a meeting in which they were criticized for "working with forces and energies [they] had no understanding about."[112] They also learned why people had been trying to disrupt the ritual: because they believed "the Baphomet energy was too dangerous to invoke."[113] Melbourne Pagan Gavin Andrews put the dispute into perspective:

> Much of the controversy centred around whether it was appropriate to present dark ecstatic rituals, with the potential to facilitate deep personal transformations, within a festival format. Others found Euphoria's presiding deity,

111. Hawthorn, "Baphomet 1999: Chaos, Controversy and Ecstasy," Euphoria website, https://web.archive.org/web/20120321045235/http://www.euphoriapagan.org/histories.html#1999.
112. Seline, quoted in Douglas Ezzy, *Sex, Death and Witchcraft: A Contemporary Pagan Festival* (Bloomsbury, 2014), 7.
113. Hawthorn, quoted in Ezzy, *Sex, Death and Witchcraft*, 6.

> Baphomet, problematic—not least due to the genderqueer associations of this deity, openly contrasting with the heteronormative—I hesitate to use the term "orthodoxy"—accepted within the Pagan scene at the time."[114]

While some Pagans at the gathering found the nature of the rite disturbing, the majority of the people who actually participated reported enjoying the ritual and the energy it generated:

> [The Baphomet Rite] was a real celebration of being alive and being human. It was more than your usual circle dance. There was a lot more raw energy, a lot more erotic elements. There was a fierceness to it, and an unrestrained passion. I saw people enjoying themselves. I saw that same sense of awe and wonder that I had seen at some other Pagan rituals when people just lost themselves in the moment, and in being magical.[115]

The ritualists were also deeply affected by the rite:

> We had so many people coming up and saying how great the ritual was. I was still awake at dawn. That was the first big ritual I had been to where we had a lot of drumming and energy like that and that ecstatic energy. People were hugging; people were standing in circle just hugging. I had not seen or felt that emotional reaction to a ritual. Heaps of people skyclad by that time. They

---

114. Cosette Paneque, "Column: Australia's Pagan Festivals," *The Wild Hunt* (blog), November 14, 2015. https://wildhunt.org/2015/11/column-australias-pagan-festivals.html.
115. "Sauvage," quoted in Ezzy, *Sex, Death and Witchcraft*, 7.

> hadn't started skyclad. It was just incredible. The whole thing was really magical from start to finish.[116]

The experience and events at the Pagan Summer Gathering prompted Hawthorn (the rite's creator) and Seline (one of the ritualists) to create the Euphoria festival. The next year, the first Euphoria was held at a site outside Melbourne, taking place in the fall during the Easter Long Weekend. Three main rituals were performed each night of the festival, with the Baphomet Rite always held on the third and final night.

Unfortunately, not much has been written about the Euphoria festival, which ran from 2000–2009. The 2005 Euphoria was documented by Australian sociologist Douglas Ezzy in his 2014 book *Sex, Death and Witchcraft: A Contemporary Pagan Festival*. Ezzy presents a fascinating analysis of the Baphomet Rite that serves as the primary resource for this chapter.[117] Another source on the rite is the Euphoria festival website, which can be accessed via the Internet Archive Wayback Machine.[118] These two resources were supplemented by interviews from the internet and personal emails with some of the ritualists. Together these sources reveal the concept of Baphomet that manifested through the performance of the Rite at the Euphoria festival.

---

116. Hawthorn, quoted in Ezzy, *Sex, Death and Witchcraft*, 8.
117. Ezzy's book is a sociological analysis of the 2005 Euphoria festival; in order to protect the identity of those involved, all names given therein are pseudonyms. For example, Ezzy identifies the festival as "Faunalia" and Baphomet Rite creator Hawthorn as "Harrison." Therefore, some of the names of people interviewed in Ezzy's book quoted and cited here are enclosed in quotation marks to signify that we do not know their real identities.
118. https://web.archive.org/web/20120321041658/http://www.euphoriapagan.org/Index.html.

Constructing the Rite

Three concepts—the witches' sabbat, ecstatic ritual, and Baphomet—form the core of the Baphomet Rite.[119] These concepts existed outside the norms of the Australian Pagan paradigm, satisfying Hawthorn's desire for the Rite to be confrontational and transformative:

> I wanted to create a rite that would challenge people's prejudices.... A lot of modern Paganism in my opinion is way too sanitized and inoffensive and not challenging to the status quo. I wanted to have an experience that was an emotional experience, that was moving and wonderful and magical.[120]

Both the sabbat's and Baphomet's association with the Christian devil also served to confront Pagans' Christian indoctrination. This was intentional on Hawthorn's part: "I get a bit impatient with Pagans when they don't let go of their Christian baggage. Pagans are scared of the devil."[121] In the rite, people would be able to confront the devil in the form of Baphomet, have the opportunity to let go of this Christian superstition, and then commune with Baphomet, replacing the discarded superstition with a positive and magical experience.

The satanic and sexual elements the rite invokes are also elements of our collective shadow. In this context, the rite is a form of Jungian shadow work, where these elements are encountered, accepted, and integrated in a ritual setting. The people running Euphoria were fully aware of this connection and suggested people

---

119. Hawthorn. "Baphomet 1999: Chaos, Controversy and Ecstasy," Euphoria website, https://web.archive.org/web/20120321045235/http://www.euphoriapagan.org/histories.html#1999.

120. Ezzy, *Sex, Death and Witchcraft*, 4.

121. Ezzy, *Sex, Death and Witchcraft*, 11.

read Robert Johnson's book *Owning Your Own Shadow: Understanding the Dark Side of the Psyche* before attending the festival.

Another important aspect of the Baphomet Rite is that it serves as a safe and sanctioned space to explore these darker themes. There is a strict and explicit code of conduct that all participants must follow while at the festival, and those in charge of the ritual take significant steps to make sure that people are fully informed of all aspects of the rite. Participants are also given permission to leave the ritual space if they feel uncomfortable with the ritual or whatever it invokes within them. Everyone involved understands that there are risks when exploring darker themes in ritual, but they also recognize the significant rewards of doing so.

The Baphomet Rite

The Baphomet Rite takes place on the third night of the festival. It begins in the afternoon with a mandatory pre-ritual workshop where each part of the ritual is explained to the participants. This allows them to give their informed consent to partake in the Baphomet Rite, which is important due to its dark and erotic nature. At the workshop, Hawthorn leads everyone in a guided meditation in which they imagine taking part in a witches' sabbat. They are taught a couple of chants that will be used in the ritual, and each person is also given a strip of white cloth.

After dinner, the ritual team goes up to the ritual site to prepare. The participants also start to prepare themselves; some change into ritual garb or costumes, while others prefer to attend skyclad. Some people engage in body painting or cover their bodies with mud or clay. They gather around the bonfire in the central courtyard in anticipation for the ritual to begin. The drumming and suspense put many participants into a light trance state conducive to ritual work.

The group is summoned around 11 p.m. They form a procession and walk toward the ritual site on a candle-lit path in the light of the full moon. The drumming continues as they advance, and the people recite one of the chants taught to them at the workshop. As they walk down the path, they are challenged along the way by ritualists representing the four elements.

People gather around a large bonfire in the center of the ritual site. When all are present, the four elemental ritualists call the quarters and cast the circle. The circle is cast widdershins (clockwise in the Southern Hemisphere) instead of the traditional direction, deosil (counterclockwise, the direction the sun appears to travel through the sky in the Southern Hemisphere) to reflect that the rite is working with the darker elements of nature.

In the next part of the rite, the participants symbolically bind their wrists with the strips of white cloth while chanting "ignorance and oppression, fear and guilt." Then they throw the bindings into the fire, symbolically releasing themselves from these negative emotions as the cloth is consumed by flames.

The main part of the rite starts when the people engage in another chant: "Let the beast without awaken the beast within." As the energy and anticipation builds, two priests perform an invocation of Baphomet. One priest wears only a white face mask, his naked body decorated with the symbols of the planets. The other priest is clad in a black robe with a Christian priest's collar, and his face is painted red with black features to mimic the face of the Christian devil.

Then the priestess emerges from the darkness, dressed as Baphomet. She wears an elaborate goat's head with a pentagram on her forehead and a lit torch between her horns. *Solve* and *coagula* are written on her arms. Bared breasts, black wings, and a large wooden phallus complete the transformation. The appearance of Baphomet has a strong emotional effect on many of the participants.

One by one, they come up to kiss the behind of Baphomet. Then the priestess, possessed by Baphomet, goes around the circle and communes with each of the participants in a nonverbal manner, grunting, growling, gesturing, sharing the energy of Baphomet. She then blesses a cup of red wine shared by all present, giving the participants a second opportunity to partake of the energy of Baphomet.

At this point, the ritual becomes less scripted and more spontaneous. Music starts, and some people begin to dance around the bonfire. Others also engage in erotic behavior and sexual activity. Later, some participate in the feast of the beast, where food is served on naked bodies and diners use their mouths to sensually kiss and even bite the human platters as they eat.

The participants revel until they get tired and crash. The few people left close the circle shortly before dawn. The rite is complete.

Euphoria's Baphomet

Like Lévi's image, Euphoria's concept of Baphomet embraces both darkness and light. Ezzy observes that within the context of the rite, Baphomet "represents the shadow selves of Western Christian culture, the repressed sexual and animalistic aspects of being human."[122] This is the shadow side of Baphomet. Baphomet also signifies the expression and integration of these primal instincts—the light side of Baphomet. This interplay between shadow and light is reflected in the three roles that Baphomet plays in the rite.

122. Ezzy, *Sex, Death and Witchcraft*, 125.

First, Baphomet functions as a stand-in for the devil, which encourages participants to confront any leftover Christian baggage that may hinder them in finding happiness and fulfillment as Pagans. This includes the Christian delusions that the material body and its sexual urges are bad or evil rather than natural and sacred. The energy of Baphomet is a catalyst that turns oppressive Christian attitudes and transmutes them, as one participant discovered:

> The Baphomet [rite] was very, very challenging to me. Some of it because of personal stuff going on … [Also] because the Catholic in me was really struggling with it. It was not something I had found any personal resolution of in my past. The first couple of Baphomet rituals that I did, I thought were stupid, because I thought, "this is just dumb." That whole thing about fighting against the whole Catholic thing. How dark is that? I had a lot of this stuff going on in my head. The getting caught up in the energy, and doing things like kissing women, which I had never done before. That came out for me in the Baphomet [rite]. It was a safe place for me to explore my own sexuality and experience some things that normally I would not get to experience, and then go away and think about how that impacted upon my life and upon my psyche.[123]

Second, Baphomet is the catalyst that frees people from oppression, both through Their presence in the rite and through the energy They give to the participants via direct communication. The act of communicating with Baphomet was often described as an extremely emotional experience:

---

123. "René," quoted in Ezzy, *Sex, Death and Witchcraft*, 102.

> When Baphomet got to me, I saw her. She actually walked past me and stopped, turned around and went, "Oooh", and came back and grabbed my hands and it was explosive. I was shaking and crying and two people [stood] beside me. I felt hands come on my shoulders, and it was like, holy fuck! I do not know these people, they are supporting me, they can obviously see that there is some deep shit going on here.[124]

Other participants were moved by the experiences they witnessed:

> The rite sweeps me away as I watch Baphomet move among the participants. He/She walks past Jade and then turns back. Standing nearby, I feel their exchange as Baphomet roars into Jade's face and third eye. Heads together, they bridge a gulf of guilt, pain and suffering. The two beings become one, screaming and roaring. This is why I am here. To see this moment.[125]

Third, Baphomet, as the primal energy of nature, represents the repressed sexual and animalistic aspects of humanity, and the rite provides an opportunity for the participants to briefly connect with this energy. The rite serves as safe space in which to express the ecstasy, eroticism, and other emotions this connection sparks within humans:

> In the ritual we were expressing raw lust. Just expressing raw lust. We start by dancing. We start by dancing with

124. "Jenny," quoted in Ezzy, *Sex, Death and Witchcraft*, 117.
125. "Impressions of a first timer, Euphoria 2005, by Rachel" from http://www.euphoriapagan.org/histories.html.

> each other. As we dance, we explore. We explore by reaching out to others, and if other people are responsive to that, then going further in that exploration. It might be touching, it might be caressing, in might be kissing, it might be more sexual and more intimate. It might be with one person, it might be with a group of people. It might be whatever happens spontaneously within that experience. It is simply honouring and allowing that aspect of our primal sexuality to be free.[126]

It is important to recognize that Euphoria was promoted as "a Gay, Lesbian, Bi, Trans/Inter-gender and Hetero friendly Neo-pagan festival" and thus served as a safe space for queer folks to express their sexuality as well:

> In the Baphomet ritual there was a lot of trust. Everybody went there being very open, with their hearts open ... I was really comfortable right through the ritual.... Seeing people fucking in circle, and transsexuals, and gay people, men and women. I have never experienced anything like that. It seemed very appropriate for the space because Baphomet is a very sensual ritual. Very much about raw sexual energy, and also mutually consenting. People were being careful about each other's boundaries.[127]

Many attendees remarked that participating in the Euphoria festival in general and the Baphomet Rite in particular was a very transformative experience, one that challenged their preconceptions and led both to self-discovery and a new perspective on life.

---

126. "Marie," quoted in Ezzy, *Sex, Death and Witchcraft*, 119.
127. "Dingo," quoted in Ezzy, *Sex, Death and Witchcraft*, 119.

Many reported becoming more accepting of their sexuality and their erotic desires.

Honoring Baphomet

Those who participate in the rite honor Baphomet but do not worship Them in the conventional sense, a distinction observed by Ezzy:

> Respecting and honouring a Pagan deity, such as Baphomet, does not mean obedience to that deity. Karen, a 42-year-old married Witch noted emphatically: "We do not worship Baphomet. We simply honour the energy. It is a very different concept." In many religious traditions worship is associated with obedience to a set of moral precepts and behavioural norms. In contrast, honouring suggests respect, but not obedience.[128]

Attendees interviewed by Ezzy described an ambivalent relationship with Baphomet, primarily because, as Ezzy states, "The relationship between participants and the deity honored is complex and ambivalent because Pagan deities do not necessarily act in the interests of humans."[129] This is especially true of Euphoria's Baphomet, for as a manifestation of the primal energy of nature, Baphomet can behave in wild and unpredictable ways. Ezzy illustrates these concepts with an excerpt from one participant with the pseudonym "Therion:"

> Baphomet is not a comfortable deity. Baphomet is not a deity that you would say to, "Here, I place my trust in you" and everything would be OK. Baphomet can hurt you, certainly not out of malice, I don't think. But there is

128. Ezzy, *Sex, Death and Witchcraft*, 128.
129. Ezzy, *Sex, Death and Witchcraft*, 128.

> always that sense that he, she may take people out of their comfort zone and that creates certain trust issues. I do not completely trust Baphomet. [But I still think that what happens in the Baphomet rite] is happening for a reason. I have got to trust that it is appropriate. I think in a way that is hearkening back to a much more Pagan view of the world where deities were not something that you trusted.[130]

These same ideas manifest in Carroll's Mass of Chaos B, where the energy of Baphomet is harnessed for magical purposes; in Wyrd and Vane's Circle of Baphomet ritual, designed to "share [their] living vision of Baphomet" via DMT; and in Vayne and Dee's Gates of Baphomet ritual, where participants share the chalice of Baphomet energy. Each ritual allows participants to commune with the energy of Baphomet, and each honors but does not worship the deity.

The Priestess of Baphomet

Seline played the Baphomet role in the rite for the first six festivals, an experience that gives her a unique perspective on the nature of Euphoria's concept of Baphomet.

When she first started preparing to take on the role of Baphomet, Seline would negotiate with Baphomet, insisting that she wanted to retain some control of her body during the rite. The fear of giving in to sexual desire despite the social consequences was a valid concern for a married woman invoking a deity associated with primal sexuality, as it was with other people involved with the rite given the ambivalent relationship between Pagans and their deities discussed above. Later, as she became more

130. "Therion," quoted in Ezzy, *Sex, Death and Witchcraft*, 128–29.

comfortable working with deity, she was able to give up more control to Baphomet without fear.

The experience of being possessed by Baphomet was very intense:

> I feel filled with god energy; it is an extremely empowering experience, it blows my mind, and I lose all awareness of mortal limitations. Even as I begin to come down from the experience and ground, the energy is still with me, filling me with a sense of awe and magick. ... Baphomet is all of us; I am just the physical container that manifests and acts as the focus for that energy at that time.[131]

In the Rite, Seline sees Baphomet functioning as both the confronter and the healer. As discussed earlier, Baphomet's first role in the rite is to force Pagans to confront their leftover Christian baggage. However, Seline points out that Baphomet also confronts people to explore and accept their darker sides:

> Mostly what people fear in Baphomet is the darkness that is within themselves. Baphomet is about balance; if we can't walk in the dark, how can we truly embrace the light? How can those who will only work in the light say that they truly know themselves?[132]

The theme of darkness and light comes up again, evoking the association between Baphomet and Jungian shadow work, the confrontation and integration of the darkness within us. This also alludes to the general theme of the Euphoria festival: to explore the darker side of Paganism.

---

131. Shelia, "An Interview with Seline," http://www.faunaliafestival.com/interview—seline.html.

132. Shelia, "An Interview with Seline."

And who is Euphoria's Baphomet, according to Seline, the priestess that worked most intimately with the deity?

> Baphomet is in all of us. To me, Baphomet is all gods, or goddesses, he is everything. He has the qualities of all the gods and goddesses. But it is just the one name.[133]

Her pantheistic viewpoint is echoed in another interview:

> "Baphomet is all, is everything, is ancient, timeless and wise, provocative, erotic and primal; it was there in the chaos when this world was created."[134]

Evidently Baphomet is far older than the sabbatic devil portrayed in the Baphomet Rite.

The last Euphoria festival was held in 2009. Interviews indicate that burnout likely brought the decade of Euphoria to an end. There are indications that the Baphomet Rite was performed a couple more times in the following decade, but no details have been forthcoming.

The Baphomet Rite brought a group of diverse witches together for a modern recreation of the witches' sabbat in which they confront and celebrate the darker elements within themselves, particularly their repressed sexual and animalistic desires. Baphomet was the confronter and the catalyst in this rite, both the shadow and the integrator of the shadow, who frees people from oppressive forces that hinder their personal and sexual development. The result was a transformative experience that fostered sexual freedom and personal development.

133. Seline, quoted in Ezzy, *Sex, Death and Witchcraft*, 152.
134. Shelia, "An Interview with Seline."

SOLVE
SOLVE
COAGULA

Chapter 8

The Lord of Earth and Rot

In 2002, Northern Tradition Pagan shaman and queer activist Raven Kaldera, who is both transgender and intersex, published a landmark book. *Hermaphrodeities: The Transgender Spirituality Workbook* is the first book to focus on spirituality for transgender people. Kaldera recounts myths from many different religions that features transgender or gender-bending deities; explores what can be learned from these myths through discussion, activities, and rituals; and interviews transgender and gender-bending folks about their spiritual beliefs and practices. *Hermaphrodeities* is also the first book to talk about Baphomet's special connection with transgender and other genderqueer folks.

A decade later, Ruth Addams, a member of Kaldera's community, compiled and published a devotional for Baphomet titled *A Gift of Maggots*. Her devotional includes six essays by Kaldera on the six aspects of Baphomet that are briefly mentioned in *Hermaphrodeities*. These essays reveal a unique perspective on Baphomet shaped by the experiences of people in a sex-positive, eclectic Pagan community.

Kaldera's Baphomet

While he appears to be quite familiar with the history of Baphomet, Kaldera's concept of Baphomet is based on experiential knowledge rather than academic study:

> It is ironic that after all of these years of learning mythology, I am studying with a deity who has no primary sources, no written mythos, who will not let me find out about him in the words of the ancients. Baphomet must be approached entirely through personal gnosis. . . .
> I believe the only things worth researching about him are the words written through inspiration, and the words spoken (often in hushed tones) to each other by those who have been granted the privilege of knowing him, if only a little.[135]

According to Kaldera, Baphomet has been around since the beginning of human settlement: ". . . he is a younger God, and he reeks of urban civilization."[136] In his "Hymn to Baphomet," Kaldera reports that when polytheism was suppressed by monotheism at the beginning of the first millennium and the old deities withdrew from the world, Baphomet stuck around.[137] Kaldera also states that Baphomet not having an established written or oral

---

135. Ruth Addams, *A Gift of Maggots: A Devotional for Baphomet* (Asphodel, 2010), 15. This quote (and others within the book) implies that the conception of Baphomet presented by Kaldera has been shaped by other people's personal experiences, probably by other people in his magical community (Ruth Addams, for example). Thus when speaking of Kaldera's Baphomet, we are referring to the concept of Baphomet gleaned from the experiences of many people (including Kaldera himself) and documented by Kaldera in print.
136. Addams, *A Gift of Maggots*, 15.
137. Addams, *A Gift of Maggots*, 4–6.

tradition like other deities is not accidental but by design, because They are "the embodiment of that which is Outside The System, and by definition history is part of The System."[138] The system is an illusion that obfuscates the Real World:

> ... while society tells everyone that it is the Real World, Baphomet's message is something quite opposite. That's not the Real World, he says. The Real World is outside that artificially constructed world. It is the world that sprouts grass and trees and cockroaches and hyenas and, sometimes, unusual mutants ... and in that Real World, it's the mutations that create all the change and the progress. The Real World honors both male and female equally, sees animal nature as no worse than human nature, and shit and humus as no less valuable than words and ideas.[139]

This outsider role is central to Kaldera's conception of Baphomet. Many of Kaldera's six aspects of Baphomet discussed below pertain to practices and people that fall outside the system. Baphomet values that which the system fears and rejects, including things like dirt, rot, excrement, and humus, and people such as freaks, sex workers, sexual deviants, and queer folk. Finally, Kaldera associates Baphomet with sexuality and sexual perversion, which is generally defined as any type of sexual behavior that falls outside the cultural and societal norms of the system.

Perhaps the most unique characteristic of Kaldera's Baphomet is that They are not only a deity of the earth but also an inhabitant:

---

138. Addams, *A Gift of Maggots*, 14–15.
139. Addams, *A Gift of Maggots*, 81–82.

> Another of his mysteries... comes from the personal gnosis of several of the transgender people who work with him. He has communicated to us that unlike other Gods, who live in their own otherworlds, he is always present here, being carried in a body. This was communicated especially strongly to the few that have had the privilege of carrying him themselves, of allowing their physical bodies to be possessed by his divine spirit. He doesn't live in "divine time", *kairos* time as the Greeks would put it; he lives right here with us.... While he is capable of possessing men or women in a pinch, what seems to be most comfortable for him is when he can possess the body of someone androgynous—in mind, in spirit, but especially physically androgynous. He goes from one to the next, and so he understands this world in a way that no other god can. He also loves this world, fiercely, and he loves humanity.[140]

Kaldera has firsthand knowledge of the phenomenon he describes—he has repeatedly experienced sudden, involuntary possession by Baphomet, discussed in more detail in the next section. This phenomena is very rare in contemporary American and European Paganism, where the invocation of a deity into a human for magical purposes usually happens on a voluntary basis in a ritual setting.

Baphomet knows humanity better than other deities because They have lived among us since the beginning of civilization. Baphomet has a special affinity for humans that share Their androgynous nature—transgender, intersex, and other gender-bending

140. Addams, *A Gift of Maggots*, 52–53.

people. Finally, Baphomet loves humanity; but, as we will see below, sometimes They have some unusual ways of expressing this love.

Six Aspects of Baphomet

In *A Gift of Maggots*, Kaldera identifies six significant aspects of Baphomet: Rex Mundi, the King of the World; Lord of Earth and Rot; Baphe Metis, Baptized in Wisdom; Secret Warrior; Lord of Perversions; and Sacred Abomination, Lover of the Whore of Babylon. While Kaldera acknowledges that other aspects certainly exist, these six aspects embody the Baphomet that he and his Pagan kin have interacted with. Let's examine each in turn.

Rex Mundi, King of the World

Baphomet's primary title is Rex Mundi, King of the World, which reflects Their unique and intimate connection to humanity and the planet:

> This is an allusion to several different traits—that he is Lord in the physical realm of flesh and earth as opposed to a faraway deity, that he became King when the worlds of the other gods pulled away and left their followers to the ravages of monotheism, that he is (in the words of some esoteric fringe Western pseudo-Sufis) a channel for the Kundalini energy of the earth, that he is a primal androgyne and thus symbolizes All.[141]

Kaldera also appends to Rex Mundi the related title of "the King of Freaks and Monsters," which Kaldera defines as "the leader of a subgroup that is outcast by the larger group, and knows that it is outcast, usually for unfair reasons they cannot help."[142] Rex

141. Addams, *A Gift of Maggots*, 81.
142. Addams, *A Gift of Maggots*, 74.

Mundi's intimate connection with humanity fosters a love for all humans regardless of their disabilities, flaws, or perversions. They are the king of freaks and monsters because They love them unconditionally, unlike society, which tends to shun or persecute them. Likewise, freaks and monsters will often fervently follow and fight for a leader who accepts and respects them for who they are. This puts Baphomet in the role of advocate for the outcast, the disenfranchised, and the undesirable—the outsiders.

Lord of Earth and Rot

Of the five elements, Kaldera connects Baphomet with the element of earth. He also characterizes Them as a "Dark God" with a specific relationship with death, a connection with "the rotting down process of the physical body... and all of the mental, emotional and spiritual situations that mirror the physical process of rot during the various birthing-and-dying cycles we go through in life.[143]

Baphomet values the role of rot in our ecosystem, the process that breaks dead matter into fertilizer. Kaldera also uses rot to describe the negative emotions and delusions that rot in our heads, things that keep us from reaching our true potential and living a happy life:

> Baphomet is connected to scavengers, especially to insects such as flies, maggots, and other life that feeds on rotting meat. In his case, he feeds on the rot in our psyches—the delusions, the old resentments, the pettiness and vengeful fantasies, the ancient rage, the unexpressed grief, the host of fears that leak out at inopportune moments, the smug patronizing superiorities designed to shore up our flagging self-esteem. These are

143. Addams, *A Gift of Maggots*, 89.

> all his meat, and his end goal is to take them away from us. However, let's be clear about the method. Filth-eaters, in the divine sense, do not just invisibly and painlessly remove these things from us. That's not the way it works. They can take those things from us, piece by piece, but the process is agonizing. It's more like major surgery than like pickpocketing.[144]

As we will see later, the painful process of clearing out the rot is an essential part of working with Kaldera's Baphomet. However, Their ultimate goal is altruistic—to free us from the rot within us that sabotages our personal evolution and happiness.

Kaldera also associates Baphomet with excrement and its "exit portal," the anus. The "primary purpose" of the anus "is letting go ... and that's also Baphomet's primary purpose—getting you to a point where you willingly let go of the things that are holding you back."[145] The power of this aspect of Baphomet comes from transforming the excrement and rot in our lives and our world into something useful:

> ... he has the power to transform shit into sacred fertilizer, and that goes for every other part of our twisted natures. When he sacralizes our internal darknesses, he doesn't just "look at it from a different perspective". He actively transforms them into their sacred purpose. Pain becomes the awareness of the pain of others and becomes empathy. Forgiveness becomes forgiveness of others and becomes compassion. Suffering becomes

144. Addams, *A Gift of Maggots*, 89.
145. Addams, *A Gift of Maggots*, 94–95.

> knowledge, and so on. He holds our shit—all of our shit—holy because he sees its potential.[146]

The specific process Baphomet uses to transform our rot and excrement is detailed later in this chapter.

Baphe Metis, Baptized in Wisdom

Another title of Baphomet is *Baphe Metis*, Greek for "Baptized in Wisdom." Kaldera states that "... the wisdom that Baphomet is baptized in is wisdom that comes from fully understanding and accepting both male and female energies within himself."[147] The verb "baptized" indicates that this wisdom is experiential, and that Baphomet's intimate, firsthand knowledge of humanity, Their embodiment of all genders and animal instincts, and Their connection with Earth all give Baphomet a unique understanding of how our world works.

The title "Baptized in Wisdom" was gleaned from nineteenth-century English antiquarian Thomas Wright's essay "The Worship of the Generative Powers in the Middle Ages in Western Europe" (1866), which repeated Hammer-Purgstall's spurious Baphomet claims discussed in chapter 1. Hammer-Purgstall gives *Baphe Metis* as the likely meaning of the name Baphomet. As we saw in chapter 3, Crowley also appropriated this term to allude to Baphomet in the Creed of the Gnostic Mass: "I confess one Baptism of Wisdom whereby we accomplish the Miracle of Incarnation."[148] Many other magicians and scholars believe that the name Baphomet is connected with wisdom.

---

146. Addams, *A Gift of Maggots*, 96.

147. Addams, *A Gift of Maggots*, 47.

148. Crowley, *Equinox* 3, 251.

Secret Warrior

As the Secret Warrior, Baphomet manipulates the world in covert ways. This makes perfect sense when you consider Kaldera's belief that when the Pagan deities were driven out, Baphomet remained, hiding outside the system dominated by monotheism. Outsiders that openly challenge the system within society are often silenced via murder, imprisonment, or exile. The best option is to work to change the system from the outside in ways that don't attract attention.

Those who work with Baphomet also tend to become secret warriors:

> Like the head of the revolutionary cell, he trains us in how to bring about change in ways that people don't expect. He shows us how to use distractions and subterfuges, to dress up Truth in a way that is tastier for people to choke down, to know our audience, to find the right tool to reach the right person, to weave a web so fine that no one notices when it closes them in. He teaches us to convince the enemy that his conversion to our cause was his own idea, and a clear sign of his obvious superiority as a person. He also teaches us to scare the hell out of people if that's the most effective action to secure your goals, although he will point out with a sly smile that it's the right tactic a lot less often than we might like.[149]

As the Secret Warrior, Baphomet helps outsiders promote change within the system. The outsiders in turn help Baphomet clear out the rot within the system, which is notoriously resistant to change. It's a mutually beneficial relationship.

149. Addams, *A Gift of Maggots*, 17–18.

Lord of Perversions

Kaldera characterizes Baphomet as a reverser, one "who turns everything on its head, makes black white, turns the world upside down, tells you everything you know is wrong."[150] This part of Baphomet is primarily expressed as the Lord of Perversions, which pushes people to discover the sacred within the profane, in things that evoke fear or disgust, such as dead bodies, dirt, rot, bodily fluids, and especially sex. Baphomet forces people to question what they feel when confronted with these things in order to reevaluate their feelings toward them, and to confront and overcome the fears that are evoked. Baphomet also benefits from this process:

> As Lord of Perversions, Baphomet also has the ability to use that which is shocking and disgusting to the repressed masses as a tool of magic. Forcing them to confront their issues around these things is a way to feed him, just as other gods feed off of anger or love. He can take those feelings and put them toward changing the world, and if you are one of his people, you can too. Where there's fear, there's power. Where the thing is that you were taught you shouldn't do (often for no good reason), there lies that which will set you free.[151]

Baphomet is also linked to what the system calls sexual perversions, such as BDSM and role-playing, which often involve forbidden practices and themes; and to sodomy, a practice that those within the system consider to be the foremost sin of sexual perversion and an act forbidden and taboo in many cultures.

150. Addams, *A Gift of Maggots*, 113.
151. Addams, *A Gift of Maggots*, 115.

To Baphomet, these perversions are natural expressions of human sexuality, acts that should be freely experienced and enjoyed.

The Sacred Abomination, Lover of the Whore of Babylon

Interestingly enough, Kaldera considers Baphomet to be a "slightly more masculine than feminine, a male-of-center androgyne," and thus refers to Baphomet as "he" rather than using non-gendered pronouns.[152] This masculine-leaning Baphomet is sometimes portrayed as having a consort, the Whore of Babalon, the Sacred Whore, "the special protector" of sex workers in general and "those who make their living from selling 'perversion' in particular, such as professional dominatrixes, transgender sex workers, etc."[153]

The concept of the Sacred Abomination appears to be derived from an uninitiated or outsider's interpretation of Crowley's writings on Baphomet. For example, in *A Gift of Maggots*, Kaldera writes:

> The origin of Babalon, the Scarlet Woman, the Whore in the Book of Revelations, is in many ways as murky and shadowy as Baphomet's own. (In some modern—meaning less than 150 years old—myths she is paired with Baphomet as his consort; in others she is paired with some nebulous personification of Chaos. When she is with Baphomet, however, she is clearly the less

---

152. Addams, *A Gift of Maggots*, 47.

153. Raven Kaldera, *Hermaphrodeities: The Transgender Spirituality Workbook* (Asphodel, 2008), 113. Note that Kaldera spells Babylon with a "y" in the title Lover of the Whore of Babylon, but uses the Thelemic spelling (Babalon with an "a") when referring to the goddess. Why Kaldera retains the Biblical spelling of Babylon in the title is not explained in the text.

> powerful of the two, although still very powerful in her own right.)"[154]

You might recall that the Creed in the Crowley's Gnostic Mass identifies Chaos as the "Father of Life," Babalon as "the Mother of us all," and Baphomet as "the Serpent and the Lion." Kaldera has interpreted this as a relationship between three different "mature" gods as opposed to Crowley's belief that Baphomet was the magical child of Chaos and Babalon, a dynamic that is not explicitly stated in the Mass. Also, Crowley identified himself with the Beast of Revelations and his female consorts with the Scarlet Woman (a title of Babalon), a relationship proclaimed in *The Book of the Law*, and Baphomet was the official O.T.O. magical name of the man with whom these Scarlet Women were performing sex magic.

In Thelema, Babalon represents both the archetypal mother and the fully liberated woman, especially in regard to her sexuality. In both the Book of Revelations and Crowley's works, Babalon is identified as the Mother of Abominations. As the Sacred Abomination and Lover of Babalon, Baphomet could be considered the sire of these abominations; it would certainly complement his role as the King of Freaks and Monsters.

Baphomet is the lover of the Whore of Babalon; not a trick, not a business transaction, but one who sees her as an entity worthy of love in her own right. Baphomet has told Kaldera, "*A whore is not a whore when I am present*," and Kaldera adds, "Bringing whores out of whore-space when they needed it, for their own sanity, [is] part of His sacred job."[155] This serves as yet another example of Baphomet loving and valuing someone denigrated and rejected by society: the whore.

---

154. Addams, *A Gift of Maggots*, 29.
155. Addams, *A Gift of Maggots*, 30.

Finally, Kaldera states that "Baphomet and Babalon are both characterized by an utter and complete lack of shame and an abundant amount of self-confidence in themselves, their effectiveness, and their sexuality."[156] These are attributes that many people lack in their lives, especially in their sex lives, and it is implied that working with these deities as a pair would serve to develop and strengthen these characteristics within oneself.

Clearing Out the Rot

Working with Kaldera's Baphomet is a challenging experience. Baphomet is an agent of transformation, and They expect their devotees to promote change within themselves, primarily by purifying themselves of the rot that sabotages their lives:

> [Baphomet's] one great overriding value seems to be Clear Out The Rot, wherever that may lie within us—festering illusions, old pain and resentments, rage slowly composting into grief, fears that choke and smother us, poisonous world views that taint our actions and sully our relationships. Regardless of one's home society or personal values, it's human nature to have those things ... and it's his nature to attack them.[157]

Clearing out the rot may happen on a voluntary basis, or Baphomet may choose to force it upon you, which usually seems to happen when you don't want to change. One way or the other, you will transform the rot in your life if you work with Baphomet.

The process of clearing out the rot has three steps. First, you must become aware of the piece of rot that needs to be dealt with.

---

156. Kaldera, *Hermaphrodeities*, 113.
157. Addams, *A Gift of Maggots*, 17.

Second, you must immerse yourself in the rot to fully experience it until you understand and accept it. Finally, you let it go and ideally find something to take its place, to fill the void so that the rot doesn't return. This process is a reversal of the traditional *solve et coagula* formula inscribed on Baphomet's arms: the rot has to coagulate so that we are fully aware of it and can fully experience it, and then it dissolves as we let the rot go.

This process is by no means pleasant and neither is Baphomet's role in it, as Kaldera describes in graphic detail:

> For the second step, we must acknowledge the rot, and wallow in it. . . . Baphomet puts his hoof on the back of our heads and rubs our face in it, again and again. We can't just pretend that it didn't happen like that, or euphemize or justify or pretty it up in our minds, or play little games about culpability or responsibility or who really is the victim here. We just breathe it in and accept it and go through the emotions we've been trying to avoid. We smell the stench of rot, we puke and cry and think we can't bear it, we flinch away but he is relentless. Back down in the muck we go, until we can just be with it. Until we can smell it without puking. Until we can see clearly how far that stench permeates. Until we have nothing left to pretend.[158]

Baphomet can be a harsh taskmaster! Kaldera admits that Baphomet gets pleasure from our pain, but he explains that They are pleased because our pain is a sign of our progress, and that Their ultimate goal is not to torment us but to foster our personal development. Baphomet benefits from this process as well—They

---

158. Addams, *A Gift of Maggots*, 91–92.

feed off the pain and energy generated from clearing out the rot and use it to fuel the various aspects and functions described in the previous section; that is, They use it to change the world.

The fact that working with Kaldera's Baphomet can be a rigorous and even painful process may be influenced by the author's own experiences. In *Dark Moon Rising: Pagan BDSM and the Ordeal Path*, Kaldera identifies himself as a serious sexual sadist whose appetites can only be satisfied by intense BDSM. He credits Baphomet for inspiring him to incorporate his sexuality (BDSM) into his Pagan spirituality, establishing what he calls the Ordeal Path in Paganism. This practice uses carefully and consensually negotiated pain, fear, and suffering to put people into altered states of consciousness, which can then be harnessed for magical workings. The process of clearing out the rot often evokes these same feelings, and the altered state that results creates a liminal space in which one may gain a different perspective of the rot that helps to let go of it.

Extreme Devotion

In the previous chapter, I briefly discussed how Pagans honor and respect their deities but do not generally worship them in the same way monotheistic religions do. However, in *Dark Moon Rising*, Kaldera describes a more intense form of devotion to deities, people who are involuntarily called to a higher form of service:

> If we study ancient history—and specifically the history and anthropology of Europe and central/western Asia—we find a very different attitude toward the Gods and spirits than modern Pagans embrace. Certain classes of priests, priestesses, and other religious workers were said to be "chosen" by their patron deity, and it was generally

> accepted that for the rare few who were chosen, there was no refusing the call. To do so would merely anger the deities in question, which could be fatal.... In some traditions, it is very much like being a slave of the deity in question.[159]

Kaldera is one of these people. He is the chosen of Hela, the Norse goddess of death. He does what she tells him to do or he suffers the consequences. One part of their arrangement involves a form of total-body divine possession:

> In this practice, part of the deity's consciousness comes down and inhabits the body of a human being, using it to walk about and interact with others. The mind of the human being in question may be completely unconscious, or in a vague, faraway state unable to move the body. It is referred to as being ridden, and thus the body-lender is known as a Horse.[160]

On occasion, Hela has "rented" Kaldera out to be ridden by other deities, including Baphomet. In the next section, we'll get a chance to look at this phenomenon from a different perspective.

The Voice of Maggots

Eclectic Pagan Ruth Addams is also a devotee of Baphomet. Baphomet has chosen her to serve; she belongs to Baphomet. They have a complicated relationship revealed in the many pieces

---

159. Raven Kaldera, *Dark Moon Rising* (Asphodel, 2006), 362.
160. Kaldera, *Dark Moon Rising*, 365–366.

published in her devotional to Baphomet, *A Gift of Maggots*.[161] Like Kaldera, Addams follows the Ordeal Path, designing and performing consensual and negotiated ordeals for other Pagans as well as seeking and arranging ordeals for herself.

In *Maggots*, Addams shares three intimate anecdotes regarding her relationship to Baphomet. The first one documents Baphomet riding two of her lovers, who do not remember the events after the fact. Later on, at a Pagan sex gathering, Baphomet comes forth to claim her, the deity riding the body of another friend of hers:

> He spoke to me. He told me to bring Him a handful of ash from the fire pit and give it to Him, I did so, and He marked me with it, claiming me as His. He spoke to me in His soft growl, calling me by the same pet name that He had twice before, a name none of the three humans involved knew about. He told me that there would be no comfort for me, that I had to be satisfied with knowing that He was watching. By this point I would have done anything that He asked of me, anything. He told me I could ask one thing of Him that night. I asked Him the privilege of hearing his name once again from his own lips. "*I am Baphomet*", He said. This time I understood.[162]

Baphomet led her into the darkness, to the edge of the field where the carcasses of butchered livestock were placed to rot. She followed, terrified that she would lose sight of him. There,

161. *A Gift of Maggots* also includes short essays from other people about their own perspectives and experiences regarding Baphomet. Unfortunately, examining these essays in depth would require quoting the majority of the published text to support much shorter bits of analysis and insight and thus are not discussed here.

162. Addams, *A Gift of Maggots*, 20.

Baphomet pushed her down on the ground and had sex with her. As he left, he informed her "that there was nothing in the dark more frightening than Him."[163] She was overcome with fear of the dark and fled.

In the second anecdote, Addams recounts how Baphomet ordered her to buy him a goat. The goat became unruly and had to be put down; Addams was to retrieve the skull to adorn Baphomet's temple. When she came to claim the skull, it was "almost fleshless" but still infested with maggots. Like many people, Addams has an aversion to insects, especially maggots. She carried the skull across a field and to Baphomet's temple space, maggots crawling on her skin. When she attempted to tie the skull up in a tree, the horn sheath separated from the skull and showered her with maggots. Two more times she tried to raise the skull and was showered with maggots. Addams recounts what she gained from this experience:

> Every time I see [the horn sheaths] I am reminded of His desire to seek out our issues and give the gift of forcing us to deal with them. Every time I see them I can feel the maggots again, and remember that I can face my fears, I can grow and be stronger than I was. Every time I hold them in my hands, I am grateful for His gift; a gift of maggots.[164]

As you can see, the title of the devotional not only alludes to this experience but also to Baphomet's role in clearing out the rot, as discussed earlier.

---

163. Addams, *A Gift of Maggots*, 21.
164. Addams, *A Gift of Maggots*, 99.

The final anecdote describes an act of devotion Addams endured in the service of Baphomet. In a series of dreams, Baphomet instructed her to create a ritual where her flesh was pierced by needles attached to fishing line, which in turn were anchored by a couple of friends. Baphomet would be present, riding a friend who volunteered to be Their horse for the ritual.

Addams's desire to serve stands out in her thoughts about the ritual:

> Please understand, there was never a doubt that I would give Him what He asked for, only doubt as to how it could be arranged. The fear that shook me over this did not include worries about whether or not it would hurt more than I could bear, or how damaged my flesh might be, nor should I worry about infections or other mundane concerns. My fear was simply that I would be unable to give Him what He asked of me. The idea of failing Him was devastating. When that fear did not consume me, I worried about the health of those who would be helping.[165]

In the ritual, Addams strained against her restraints to approach Baphomet, strained until they tore out of her skin and she fell, bloodied, at Their feet. Addams was pleased that she had given Them what They wanted. "He had come for me again, to receive a gift I had offered."[166]

In addition to her anecdotes, Addams also contributed numerous poems and prayers that express her fervent devotion to Baphomet. Many of them mention the aspects of Kaldera's

---

165. Addams, *A Gift of Maggots*, 134–35.
166. Addams, *A Gift of Maggots*, 136.

Baphomet described earlier. She also describes the many trials and sacrifices she endured as a possession of Baphomet. So, what does she get out of her relationship with Baphomet?

> I am involved with Baphomet because It came for me and told me I was Hers. I agreed with Him gratefully.
>
> Baphomet feels like home to me, where I belong, my "safer space." This is my place in the world. The things They ask of me by way of service are things that benefit the disenfranchised, benefit Its children, benefit me. Nothing that She has asked me has damaged me, but the things He has asked have frequently led me down paths of healing and growth, even when I could not see it at the time.
>
> Baphomet recognizes me for who I am, even seeing me far more clearly than any human could, and accepts me and values me. Many in this world see me, and do not find any value in me.
>
> I was watching the TV show *Interview With the Vampire* today and heard the words "I serve a God. It is my honour to serve." Honestly, I could list a million things, but it truly all comes down to that feeling. Baphomet does me honour by accepting my service; in doing so, They show me my own value, and who am I to argue with Deity?[167]

An examination of her poems and prayers reveals that Baphomet is a source of strength and insight for Addams. Baphomet has instilled in her a sense of humility that has increased her awareness of the world around her and her small yet significant place within it. They have taught Addams to find value in people and

167. Online interview with Ruth Addams, October 2022.

things that others do not. It is clear that Addams's relationship with Baphomet has helped her become a better person.

Kaldera's Baphomet has an intimate connection with the earth and humanity, and is a deity characterized as an outsider that promotes inclusion and acceptance of people outside the norms of society and culture. Kaldera and Addams also explore the sexual side of Baphomet, particularly Their connection to queer folk and alternative sexuality. Finally, Kaldera describes a rigorous yet rewarding process of working with Baphomet to remove the rot that interferes with our personal development and happiness.

Kaldera and Addams show us a different side of working with Baphomet, offering a glimpse of what extreme devotion can look like. And while their devotion to Baphomet may be more extreme than some people may be comfortable with, it has also given them significant insight into the nature of Baphomet that few have achieved.

PART THREE

MAGIC

Chapter 9

The Three Faces of Baphomet

In part one of this book, we covered the history of the development of Baphomet, and part two examined various esoteric conceptions of Baphomet and how people work with Them. In part three, we move from analysis to practice. While the material presented in this chapter is influenced by the information revealed in the first two parts of the book, much of the rest of the material comes from my personal work with Baphomet. Nonetheless, if one or more of the conceptions of Baphomet described in part two appeals to you, I encourage you to research them and add their knowledge and insight to your own interactions with this deity.

I wasn't working with Baphomet when I started writing this book, but I soon found that you can't write an esoteric book about a deity without them getting involved. They charged me with the task of making Them more accessible to Pagan practitioners, revealing more about Their characteristics, Their purpose, and how to work with Them. Part three is the result.

While there are some significant differences among the various conceptions of Baphomet I have analyzed in this book, they are all just different perspectives of the same deity. The common characteristics found across these different conceptions reveal Baphomet's true nature.

For example, most conceptions give Baphomet an intimate and unique connection with the earth. For Lévi, Baphomet represented the astral light that was found in all living beings. Carroll refined this idea by casting Baphomet as the spirit of the life force of the planet Earth, a concept further fleshed out by Wyrd, Vayne, and Dee. Euphoria's Baphomet Rite is based on modern Pagan rituals that honor and celebrate our connection to the earth. Finally, Kaldera gave Baphomet the titles of King of the World and Lord of Earth and claimed that They lived among the inhabitants of the planet. There are also many other, more subtle connections between Baphomet and the earth that may be discovered through research and meditation.

An analysis of the common elements of these conceptions reveals that the personality of Baphomet has three primary faces that both define who They are and present ways in which one can work with Them. These three faces of Baphomet are the Spirit of the Earth, the Outsider, and the Transmuter. As Baphomet is a deity associated with sex and sexuality, each face also includes a specific sexual component as well. These are three faces of a single complex deity, and like the faces of our own personality, they overlap and intersect in many ways. Keep in mind that Baphomet may have other faces not listed here.

First Face: The Spirit of the Earth

Baphomet is the egregore of the element of Spirit within Earth's biosphere, and therefore the Spirit of the Earth is connected with all living things. The animistic nature of the biosphere means that They are also connected with the inorganic elements needed to support life, such as air, water, and soil. In the same context, the Spirit of the Earth rules over the five elements within the biosphere, symbolically indicated by the pentagram on Baphomet's forehead.

As the Spirit of the Earth, Baphomet first emerged around four billion years ago when life began on this planet, making Them a truly ancient deity. As the oldest of the three faces, the Spirit of the Earth is the primary face of Baphomet. Their age and experience have made Them very wise, leading people to associate Baphomet with wisdom.

For the first time in billions of years, one species of mammal has grown to dominate the planet: humans. At first, we lived in harmony with the earth, but as we multiplied and evolved, we began to have a detrimental effect on the biosphere ... and Baphomet. In the nineteenth century, the damage to the biosphere became so severe that the Spirit of the Earth began to reveal Themselves to humanity in an effort to stop our destruction of the planet. Baphomet seeks to address this situation by reconnecting humanity with the earth using the five elements, a process governed by Their Transmuter face, as discussed below.

The sexual component of the Spirit of the Earth deals with fertility and the instinct to reproduce found in all life forms. As creation and destruction are complements in the natural order of the world, the Spirit of the Earth is also associated with death and decay. Finally, the Spirit of the Earth is commonly identified with Nature.

Second Face: The Outsider

One of the reasons there is so little information on Baphomet is that Baphomet is an Outsider. Since the beginning of civilization,

Baphomet has preferred to remain outside the system of human society and culture. Even today, most of the living world connected to the Spirit of the Earth still lies outside the settlements of humans.

The Outsider knows that the system must continually change to avoid stagnation and rot, and yet the system often resists change. To get around this resistance, Baphomet works from outside the system to change it, usually in subtle yet effective ways. This impulse for change is not nihilistic; the Outsider seeks to change the system, not destroy it.

Powerful corporate and political entities within the system currently resist most efforts to fight human-caused climate change, usually citing financial and ideological reasons. Like an ostrich with its head in the sand, these entities have ignored increasing global temperatures and extreme weather even as these phenomena have caused billions of dollars of damage to world economies and disrupted the lives of many millions of people. The situation is dire and the system is too slow to change, meaning it is up to those outside the system to lead the fight to save our planet.

The Outsider values and supports those who live or work outside the system. It has a special affinity for those who are forced to live outside the system, including racial, cultural, sexual, and spiritual minorities. The numerous Satanic concepts of Baphomet that manifest in our world are also reflections of the Outsider face.

While working with the Outsider might seem appealing to solitary practitioners, Baphomet encourages those outside the system to form groups and communities to promote awareness and change and to offer support to others like themselves. If outsiders truly wish to save the planet, they will have to come together to do so.

The Androgyne

The androgyne aspect of Lévi's Baphomet was originally a socialist and alchemical symbol; in the twenty-first century it has become a sexual representative of the entire spectrum of gender identity and gender expression. The Spirit of the Earth has witnessed the sexual intercourse and reproduction of every living thing on the planet, especially humans, and this wisdom and insight into sex is revealed through Their androgyne aspect.

Humans have the most complicated mating rituals and sexual habits of any animal on the planet. Unfortunately, religious and cultural taboos have also made humans the most sexually frustrated and confused animal on the planet. The role of the androgyne is to help humanity develop safe and healthy sexual relationships with other humans. The androgyne may also be called upon to help people understand and empathize with people with different gender identities and expressions.

The androgyne aspect is connected to the Outsider face for two reasons. First, to the majority of the world, gender is still a strictly binary affair, which is at odds with the gender spectrum that Baphomet represents, and many of those who do not conform to binary gender roles are persecuted or ostracized. Second, the healthy exploration and expression of sexuality is usually discouraged by societal and cultural norms.

The androgyne has a special affinity for people who are genderqueer, and They serve as the patron of queer folk in general and transgender and intersex folks in particular. The Androgyne is also the patron of sex workers, those who use their sexuality to earn a living, and sacred whores, who use their sexuality to heal others.

Third Face: The Transmuter

The Transmuter is the alchemical face of Baphomet, which facilitates the personal change required to heal humanity and reconnect them with the planet. This is indicated by the words *solve* and *coagula* written on Baphomet's arms, terms that describe the general process of alchemy.

The meaning of the term "alchemy" has changed over time. Originally, alchemy was primarily concerned with the transmutation of physical materials such as metals and plants. After physical alchemy gave birth to modern chemistry during the eighteenth century, it became one of the occult sciences of the nineteenth century and focused on the spiritual transmutation of the practitioner. In the mid-twentieth century, Swiss psychoanalyst Carl Jung (1875–1961) incorporated alchemy into analytical psychology, in which the symbols of alchemy became keys to promoting the psychological transmutation of the patient in a process called individuation. The rise of Neopaganism in the late twentieth century led to renewed interest in alchemy, particularly a blend of spiritual and psychological alchemy. This modern psycho-spiritual alchemy is the dominion of the Transmuter.

The Transmuter face seeks to change humanity through a process called elemental alchemy. By reconnecting us to the natural world through the five elements, They hope to make us more aware of our destructive behavior, so that we may change our ways and learn to live in harmony with the planet. Using elemental alchemy, the Transmuter also seeks to help us heal and grow as individuals by addressing personal elemental imbalances.

The sexual component of the Transmuter is sex magic, which is considered by some to be a form of alchemy. Sex magic harnesses the energy of the orgasm to power magical operations. It also has a physical component, where magically charged sexual fluids are consumed by the people involved or used for magical purposes.

The Powers of Baphomet

Call upon Baphomet as the Spirit of the Earth for strength, resilience, growth, and adaptability (characteristics of life); wisdom; fertility and reproduction; and natural death and decay. Baphomet inspires and supports those outsiders who desire to improve the system or to subvert it, and offers aid to those oppressed by the system. The androgyne aspect will help anyone of any sexual orientation who wishes to understand and explore their sexuality as well as to achieve both pleasure and satisfaction in their sexual endeavors. Baphomet the Transmuter is the patron of magicians, who seek to cause changes in themselves and in the world. Baphomet may also be called upon for assistance with elemental alchemy and sex magic. Finally, we may call upon Baphomet for support in any action that furthers Their environmental agenda.

The Icon of Baphomet

The characteristics of the three faces of Baphomet are present in Lévi's image. As a whole, his image represents the Spirit of the Earth. Specifically, the connection with the element of spirit is indicated by the torch above Baphomet's head and the upright pentagram on Their forehead, with spirit crowning the elements. The pentagram is placed at Baphomet's third eye, the organ of spiritual perception and insight. Baphomet's connection with the earth is indicated by the symbolism relating to its inhabitants: humans (torso and arms), mammals (goat), birds (wings), fish and reptiles (scales). Baphomet sits on a cube, a solid figure associated with alchemical salt and earth.

Lévi's Baphomet

The Outsider is represented by the goat features of Baphomet, as the goat is associated with Satan, the adversary of the divine system in Christian mythology. Baphomet is an androgyne with breasts and symbolic genitalia; the androgyne is also an alchemical symbol associated with the Transmuter. The alchemical term *solve* is written on Baphomet's right arm, pointing upward because the processes of separation and dissolution make substances lighter, while the left arm with *coagula* written on it points downward, because coagulation and solidification makes substances heavier.

From an astronomical perspective, the sphere underneath the cubic throne has been associated with planet Earth by modern scholars, and the figure of Baphomet is throned upon the planet as the Spirit governing Earth's biosphere. The two celestial bodies that directly affect life in the biosphere are present: the moon revolves around the earth/Baphomet in waxing and waning forms, while the torch above Their head represents the fire and heat of the sun.

The Nature of Baphomet

Baphomet is different than most deities we are familiar with. Deities are usually created by humans to explain natural phenomena and/or to be personifications of the human condition. To separate themselves from the human experience, our deities usually reside in heavenly realms or dark underworlds on the etheric plane. Because deities are human constructs, their power is determined primarily by the number of people that believe in them. Belief equals energy, so the more people there are who believe in a deity, the more power it will have at its disposal. Another source of power is the deities' objective identity on the material plane, their attributes and myths as well as temples or other material icons of worship or power.

In contrast, Baphomet is the egregore of the biosphere, a deity made up of the life force of everything on the planet. They are bound to the planet Earth; They exist in us and all around us; and They connect everything on the planet. They derive Their power from the collective life force of all beings on the planet, regardless of whether or not these beings believe in Baphomet. Finally, Baphomet has had very little objective identity on the material plane until very recently, and thus very little is known about Them.

Despite what Lévi and others may claim, Baphomet is not a pantheistic deity in the conventional sense, in that Baphomet is not identical to the universe; Baphomet is the spirit of the life force of planet Earth, which is essentially one point in our virtually infinite universe. However, one might consider Baphomet pantheistic in the biological sense, in that They represent the egregore of all biological life that we currently know to exist in the universe, especially the human life-forms that created universal gods and goddesses as well as the scientific instruments that allow us to see beyond our own solar system. If you are all life, including the life that creates all spiritual systems and can truly perceive the universe, then you are, in a sense, pantheistic.

Baphomet is not omnipotent. Baphomet cannot change the laws of physics, though They may appear to bend them once in a while. Baphomet can strengthen or weaken the life force of organisms, but They do not control the cycle of life and death. In other words, Baphomet is neither a hit man nor a reanimator.

Baphomet has come forth to restore the balance between humanity and the earth. They seek to accomplish this goal by helping humanity evolve into more environmentally conscious and enlightened beings. The three faces of Baphomet work to accomplish these goals on three levels: the Spirit of the Earth creates change on a global or biospheric level, the Outsider facilitates change on a societal and community level, and the Transmuter promotes change on an individual level. Working with Baphomet usually begins on the individual level, because creating change on the community and global level is easier if we first create change ourselves and establish our own relationship with the Earth.

Baphomet is a deity of evolutionary change. If you are afraid of or resistant to making changes in your life, Baphomet is not the deity for you. Baphomet likes to push those stuck on the path to evolution, an experience that may not always be pleasant. Yet while evolutionary change can be uncomfortable, it usually leads to new perspectives of knowing and being. More importantly, if we do not change the way we live soon, some parts of our biosphere will become inhospitable and even uninhabitable, and we will be forced to drastically change the way we live anyway.

Solve
Coagula

Chapter 10
Working with Baphomet

All living beings are connected to Baphomet; we live within Baphomet and we are all part of Baphomet. To start working with Baphomet, all we have to do is acknowledge this connection. Once a relationship is established, we can work with Baphomet to improve ourselves and our relationship with the planet.

Keeping a Record

When engaging in exercises of self-improvement and magic, you must keep a record of your experiences and results. It's an important tool for remembering what happened, monitoring your progress, and reflecting on your feelings and thoughts. A journal is essential, whether digital or physical in nature.

When performing meditations, doing magical work, or communicating with Baphomet or other entities, make an audio recording of the session so you can remember what was said and what you experienced. Every smartphone has a simple digital recording app built into it. Remember to put your phone in airplane mode when recording events and conversations so you won't be interrupted, and to vocalize everything you hear and experience, especially the other side of any conversations you might have. When you are done recording, don't forget to turn airplane mode off.

Grounding

Knowing how to ground yourself is essential if you're doing any kind of energy work. Grounding involves moving excess and/or negative energy down into the Earth by establishing a connection with the Earth. Ideally, this exercise should be done at the beginning and end of any of the exercises and rituals in this book. It is especially important to ground after energy and ritual work to release any excess energy you may have accumulated during the working and to help bring you back to normal consciousness.

To ground, stand or sit with your feet firmly on the ground, and breathe slowly and deeply. Imagine roots coming out of your feet and growing into the earth. When you exhale, visualize the excess energy and/or negative energy in your body being drawn down into the earth; when you inhale, visualize elemental energy coming up from the earth, through the roots in your feet, and into your body. Continue this visualization until you feel calm and centered.

Offerings

Baphomet does not desire material offerings. As the Spirit of the Earth, They are already a part of anything you could offer to Them, such as food, flowers, precious stones, and other items. Baphomet prefers that people perform acts of service as offerings, particularly actions that serve Their environmental and evolutionary purpose. In other words, Baphomet doesn't want you to give things to Them—They want you to do things for Them.

Baphomet will often help you in return for certain acts of service, including assistance with making changes that promote personal evolution or that improve your relationship with the planet. On some occasions, you may possess a skill that Baphomet values and desires to employ for a particular goal. Working with Baphomet often involves negotiating with Them to reach an arrangement beneficial for everyone—that's why communicating with Baphomet is an important part of working with Them. Outside of negotiating terms with Baphomet, performing an act of service in Baphomet's name is easy—simply state your intention to do so and They will hear you.

Magical Tools

Baphomet is a magical minimalist—an altar with an icon of Baphomet on it is all you really need to work with this deity. Anything else you place upon the altar should be an item that symbolize your personal relationship with Baphomet. Besides a statue of Baphomet, I have only two things on my altar: a molar from my mouth that I gave to Baphomet, signifying that Baphomet owns a piece of me; and a battered clear quartz crystal, a piece of the earth that I have carried with me since childhood, symbolic of a lifelong relationship with the earth. That's it. You may decorate your altar however you wish, but don't confuse a Pagan altar with a Satanic altar—we're not going for dark and spooky antinomian aesthetics here, unless that truly represents your relationship with Baphomet.

The same concept applies to other magical tools. A deity connected to everything in the biosphere has no "official" incense, precious stone, herbs, etc. If you want to use incense in your work, choose one that reminds you of Baphomet and/or your relationship with Them—and keep in mind that just because someone throws together an incense blend and labels it "Baphomet" doesn't mean it will work for you. Likewise, if you prefer to use a wand or athame to direct energy in ritual work, buy or make one that reflects your relationship with the deity. If you use tools, they should ideally serve as physical links to Baphomet.

I have used only one magical tool in my work with Baphomet, a hematite ring that hangs on the upright two fingers of the raised arm of my Baphomet statue. I consider it to be a part of my altar statue, and when I put it on my finger it strengthens my magical link with Baphomet. I frequently used this ring when I first started talking with Baphomet, as my connection to the deity was not as strong as it is now. I still use the ring on occasion when I feel the need to boost our connection, usually when I'm having trouble focusing due to fatigue, anxiety, or some other factor, yet still want to converse with Baphomet.

Baphomet wants you to do magic, and They usually aren't fussy about how you do it. The one exception is that sometimes Baphomet instructs people to make or acquire something for Them, often as part of an effort to teach them something important. Ruth Addams's anecdote in chapter 8 about acquiring a goat skull for her Baphomet altar is a good example. However challenging they may be, these opportunities for growth should always be embraced.

Meditation

The first way to start working with Baphomet is through meditation. Meditation is the easiest way to work with Them because it requires no equipment, only a comfortable place to sit or recline in a quiet space.

Many people find meditation difficult, mainly because they've been taught that meditation is all about working to stop the constant dialogue in our heads, to achieve a peaceful "no-mind" state that leads to enlightenment and spiritual bliss. This is but one form of meditation, and it usually takes practitioners months or years to achieve the "no-mind" state for any significant period of time. Other forms of meditation are much easier.

Simply put, meditation is a process in which you stop paying attention to the world around you to focus your attention on the world within you. There are two types of meditation, passive and active. Passive meditation is used to focus and quiet the mind. Mindfulness meditation, where you focus on your breathing and avoid thinking about anything else, is a prime example of passive meditation. Active meditation focuses on a subject or idea in order to gain insight and information. Contemplating the meaning of a spiritual symbol or exploring how you feel about a new job is an example of active meditation. Meditation can also put you in a trance state, which makes it easier to talk with spiritual entities.

Breathing is an important part of meditation. Long, deep breaths help to relax the body and the mind. In particular, a long exhale activates the parasympathetic nervous system, which decreases your heart rate, lowers your blood pressure, and relaxes your muscles.

Baphomet is the divine force that connects all living things upon the planet. All living things are dependent on the earth for their survival. It is to the earth we go to find Baphomet's wisdom.

Wisdom of Baphomet Meditation

1. Prior to beginning this meditation, determine what it is that you seek wisdom about and formulate it as a statement of intent. You can use phrases like "I seek to gain a better understanding of …" or "It is my will to know …" If

you are doing this meditation to connect with Baphomet, say so.

2. Find a place where you may lie down undisturbed. Close all the blinds and turn off most of the lights. A dark room is best, but it doesn't have to be pitch black. Lie down, get comfortable, close your eyes, and breathe deeply.
3. Imagine that you are lying outside on the ground in a familiar place, like the grass in your backyard or a favorite park. Now imagine that your body begins to sink into the earth. It sinks a couple of feet until you are completely buried. You feel the weight of the earth all around you, yet you can still breathe; when you inhale, the smell of rich soil fills your lungs. Under the earth, it is peacefully silent. In this place you feel connected to all of Earth's life forms. Contemplate this feeling for as long as you wish before making your appeal:

   Baphomet, Spirit of the Earth, share with me your wisdom.
   Baphomet, Outsider, reveal the insight that comes from without.
   Baphomet, Transmuter, transform my ignorance into wisdom.

4. Declare your statement of intent, then wait for a response. Most people describe hearing a voice inside their head that is not their own, but others may hear a voice coming from the earth surrounding them. If you have any doubt about who you are talking to, vibrate or intone the name

Baphomet three times. Note that terrestrial spirits generally either respect or fear Baphomet and do not usually interfere with people working with Them.

5. Converse with Baphomet until you have the answers to your questions. When you are done, thank Baphomet for sharing Their wisdom with you. Then imagine your body rising out of the earth, looking just as it did when you began the meditation.
6. Open your eyes, ground yourself, and record the experience in your journal.

Theurgy

Another way to start working with Baphomet is to use some basic techniques of theurgy to establish a relationship. Theurgy means "god-working" in Latin; the god-working you are going to do is dedicate a small space in your home to Baphomet by invoking the essence of Baphomet into a statue. While Baphomet exists everywhere around us and within us, for practical purposes it is helpful to have something to focus your attention on when working with the deity.

To start, acquire an image or statue of Baphomet and find a private place to set up an altar as discussed in the previous section. Next, write an invocation of Baphomet. Think of it as an invitation for the deity to inhabit the icon on your altar. A basic deity invocation starts with addressing the deity you wish to work with (Baphomet), what you want from them (invoke Them into a statue), and why you want to do it (to honor and to talk with Them). This is often followed by a series of epithets, descriptive statements that further identify the deity you're working with, like

"Goat-headed one, come forth!" or "Bearer of the torch of illumination and intelligence! Thee, Thee I invoke!" For example, this is the invocation I used when I set up my first Baphomet altar:

I call upon thee, O Baphomet, the personification of all life on this planet!

I invite you to come forth and dwell in this sacred statue that I may converse with thee and gain wisdom and understanding.

Baphomet, ever present! Thee, Thee I invoke!

Goat-headed one, who looks over the mountains and whose hooves stand on the deepest parts of the Earth! Thee, Thee I invoke!

Bearer of the torch of illumination and intelligence! Thee, Thee I invoke!

Manifestation of all genders! Thee, Thee I invoke!

Solve et Coagula! Creator and Destroyer! Thee, Thee I invoke!

Icon of balance and equilibrium! Thee, Thee I invoke!

Horned one, potent, powerful, peaceful! Thee, Thee I invoke!

Where the script says "Thee, Thee I invoke!" I made the Sign of the Enterer, a magical gesture used by magicians to direct energy, which I employed to fill the statue with the energy of Baphomet. Based on what I know now, the gesture probably wasn't necessary, as Baphomet doesn't need energy to manifest—They just need an invitation. You're welcome to use this invocation; however, crafting your own invocation will be more effective, as it will reflect your personal understanding of Baphomet.

The final step is to perform a short ritual to invoke the essence of the deity into the statue.

Baphomet Icon Invocation Ritual

1. Open the ritual as you see fit according to your magical tradition or beliefs. You may banish or create a magical circle if you desire, but it is not technically necessary—you already live within the body of Baphomet, so you don't need to create a separate sacred space to work with Them.
2. Read your invocation of Baphomet with a strong and energetic voice while focusing on the icon on your altar. Visualize the energy of Baphomet as a white light concentrating in and energizing your icon as you speak.
3. After you finish reading the invocation, you should feel the presence of Baphomet. Stop and listen for a response. You should be able to hear the deity speak to you in your head; sometimes the voice appears to come from the icon on the altar. Thank Baphomet for coming, introduce yourself, and engage in conversation.
4. When you're done talking with Baphomet, thank Them for their help. Perform a closing ritual if necessary. You don't need to banish, but you should ground yourself after you're done. Record the experience in your journal.

Now that you have initiated a relationship with Baphomet, you may talk to Them whenever you desire. Stand or sit in front of your altar, ground yourself and relax, and then call upon Them until They answer.

Invocation

The ultimate act of connecting with Baphomet involves invoking the deity into yourself. The primary reason for doing so is to unite your consciousness with that of Baphomet. Unification with Baphomet has many benefits—it may bring wisdom, healing, or insight. Most importantly, this unification allows one to obtain Baphometic consciousness, the ability to perceive the interconnectedness of all things on the planet and to feel the ebb and flow of the living biosphere. Another reason for invocation is to use the energy of Baphomet to empower a magical operation.

The first step in undertaking an invocation of Baphomet is to determine if you should even attempt it at all. Working with Baphomet in this way has its risks. The intense energy of the invocation may be too much for you to manage. It is also possible that you may not yet possess the skill or knowledge to successfully complete the invocation, or it just may not be the right time in your life to invoke Baphomet. You may use tarot cards or other means to determine whether to invoke, but the best way is to ask Baphomet Themself. Perform the Wisdom of Baphomet Meditation described earlier, using a statement of intent like, "I seek insight on invoking you into my body."

There are many ways to invoke Baphomet. The technique we will use is modeled after a Golden Dawn practice known as the assumption of godforms. In Golden Dawn initiations, each temple officer has a specific Egyptian god-form associated with it. Before the ritual starts, each officer assumes their godform, merging with them for the purpose of initiating a candidate. It's one of the things that makes their initiation rituals so powerful! It doesn't require an elaborate costume or entheogens, but it does require developing skills of visualization to pull it off. (Exercises for developing visualization skills can be found in many books on magic, including Carroll's *Liber Null & Psychonaut*.)

Start by selecting an image or statue of Baphomet to study. You may use Lévi's image, one from another book, your favorite statue of Baphomet, or even an image you have created yourself. Practice visualizing this image of Baphomet until it becomes easy to do. This may take days or weeks depending on your ability.

The invocation ritual requires a room where you will be undisturbed. Many people find it easier to visualize in a dimly lit room. If you have something that you associate with Baphomet, such as incense or a ring, you should bring it into the ritual. Set up two chairs facing each other, one for you and one for Baphomet. Finally, don't forget to use your phone to record any conversation that occurs during the ritual.

Invocation of Baphomet Ritual

1. Open your temple as you see fit. As mentioned above, banishing or creating a magical circle is not necessary to work with Baphomet. Activate your physical links to Baphomet: light incense, put on jewelry, et cetera.
2. Sit down and visualize Baphomet in the chair in front of you while vibrating Their name. As you vibrate "Baphomet," see this representation growing stronger, becoming more life-like. You may also recite an invocation of Baphomet if you desire, but it must be memorized so you are not distracted from your visualization.
3. When you see and feel that Baphomet is present before you, turn around and merge your body with that of the deity. Assume the attitude of Baphomet at this time, raising your right arm with two fingers pointing up and extending your left arm downward with two fingers pointing down. Feel

yourself become one with Baphomet, Their energy, and Their consciousness. State to the world, "I am Baphomet!" If desired, you may also utter a series of epithets that identify you as Baphomet, such as, "I am Baphomet, the goat-headed deity!" or "I am Baphomet, bearer of the torch of illumination and intelligence."

4. If the invocation is successful, you will likely experience Baphometic consciousness, the gnosis that you are connected to everything that lives through Baphomet. Your ego will temporarily disappear and your consciousness will expand to fill the biosphere.
5. Commune with Baphomet or perform your magical operation.
6. When you are finished, you must return to normal individual consciousness—you must separate yourself from Baphomet. In *The Book of Baphomet*, Nikki Wyrd advises us that "the standard most effective method is to state your name and address, repeating until you are totally convinced of your individuality once more."[168] A banishing ritual is not really appropriate here, as you cannot banish Baphomet! A deity invocation fills your body with a significant amount of powerful energy, so make sure to ground out when you are done. Eating after the invocation will also help you ground out.

Once you have established a relationship with Baphomet, They will work with you to heal yourself and develop a healthier con-

168. Wyrd and Vayne, *The Book of Baphomet*, 221.

nection with the earth. One way to accomplish these goals is to use the process of elemental alchemy presented at the end of this book. Before we get into elemental alchemy, though, let's examine the five elements and how they manifest in our lives.

GOAT
SOLVE
COAGULA

Chapter 11
The Five Elements

All entities within the biosphere are composed of a combination of five elements. All five elements are required for an entity to exist and function; the removal of just one of the elements would cause an entity to disintegrate. Thus, all elements are equal, as all elements are important to life; no one element is more important than another. From the biospheric perspective, elements have no hierarchy and no gender.

The five elements are philosophical concepts with qualities based in part on their physical characteristics. In our lives, elements usually manifest as balanced, deficient (not enough elemental influence), or dominant (too much elemental influence).[169] The difference between the normal elemental flux of daily life and an unbalanced element is determined by examining the intensity and frequency of the problem, with significantly high or low intensity and/or frequency usually indicating an imbalance.

169. The idea that elements within us can manifest as balanced, deficient, or dominant is adopted from *Ecoshamanism* by James Endredy (Llewellyn, 2005), 100–107.

For example, it's normal to feel angry when you are passed up for a promotion at work. If you get so angry that you trash your office, you have a problem with intensity; if you feel angry at work all day and come home every day feeling angry, you have a problem with frequency; both indicate the presence of too much fire. On the other hand, if not getting a job that should have been rightfully yours doesn't even affect you (low intensity) and you don't feel any passion or ambition for work (low frequency), you may have too little fire.

Table 3
Correspondences of the Five Elements

Element	Color	Direction	Tarot Suit	Symbols
Fire	Red	South	Wands	
Air	Yellow	East	Swords	
Water	Blue	West	Cups	
Earth	Green/ Black	North	Disks	
Spirit	White	Center	Trumps	

Fire is the realm of creation and energy, and the primary physical characteristics of fire are heat and light. The spark that starts a fire is associated with the spark of creativity, inspiration, and creation. The light that fire provides associates the element with illumination and insight. In the natural world, fire spreads very quickly, and thus the element is associated with speed, drive, activity, assertiveness, and movement. Fire's ability to remove impurities from metal and bacteria from food link it with purification. Water may be the realm of emotions in general, but emotions associated with energy and heat are often attributed to fire like passion, enthusiasm, excitement, anger, and rage.

When we are fire-deficient, we lack the energy to go out and live life. We may have trouble asserting ourselves or taking action when necessary. We may feel lazy or tired all the time. We might lack creativity, insight, and passion, and others might consider us boring and predictable as a result.

Fire-dominant people have too much energy, and this energy often builds up pressure within us until it erupts and rage, aggression, and other hostile emotions burst forth. We may feel restless, and often feel the urge to always be doing something. We can be quick to take on new projects or responsibilities but have trouble completing tasks, especially when a new project or idea captures our attention. We may have trouble relaxing or resting.

Air is the realm of thought and communication. Like air, thoughts are invisible yet have tangible effects; related qualities include intellect, knowledge, concentration, analysis, logic, and reason. Air is the medium for three of our senses, sight (light waves), hearing (sound waves), and smell (scent), and is thus associated with communication, understanding, perception, and learning. Air is associated with the conscious mind, the primary producer and processor of thoughts.

The air-deficient lack ideas; we may come across as simple-minded or disinterested. We may have trouble concentrating or thinking things through, and we often lack common sense. We may have trouble communicating with others.

When we are air-dominant, we tend to be lost in our thoughts, much like the stereotypical absent-minded professor. We may act in a detached, insensitive, or selfish manner toward others. We may overanalyze situations and have difficulty making decisions.

Water is the realm of emotion and intuition. The characteristics of water tend to be based more on metaphorical comparisons to the mind than physical qualities. Emotions flow, surge, and ebb like water. Some emotions are pleasant, such as joy, pleasure, satisfaction, love, and sensuality, while others are unpleasant, such as fear, sadness, depression, grief, and loneliness, but all are part of the vast ocean of emotions that are necessary to the human experience. Water is associated with the unconscious mind, the unseen depths below the surface of the conscious mind. Emotions and emotional control are necessary for relating to other people, associating water with friendships and relationships and the emotions associated with them, like sympathy, compassion, intimacy, cooperation, jealousy, and obsession. While some people (like Jung) attribute intuition to fire, intuition is usually experienced as a feeling (not a spark) and comes from the unconscious, thus belonging to realm of water. As the universal solvent, water is associated with cleansing.

When we are water deficient, we may often have trouble expressing our feelings or empathizing with other people. Friendships and relationships may not come easily to us. We may come across as cold or unfeeling to others. We don't get much pleasure or satisfaction out of life.

Water-dominant people can be moody, moving from one emotional extreme to another, ecstatic one minute and depressed the next. We may feel emotions so intensely that we become overwhelmed by them. Our strong emotions may cloud our judgment and compel us to act impulsively without considering the effects or consequences of our actions.

Earth is the realm of the physical world. The solidity of earth provides stability and structure; related qualities include resilience, strength, and endurance. The soil nurtures plants and animals that serve as our main source of food, which associates earth with growth, fertility, agriculture, prudence, and abundance. Earth is also associated with physical health, which is influenced by diet and environment. Many objects associated with wealth come from the earth, such as gold, silver, and precious gems, thus connecting earth with commerce, money, employment, and materialism. Finally, light cannot penetrate the solidity of earth, and thus earth is associated with darkness.

When we are deficient in earth, we often feel unstable and ungrounded. We may have trouble settling down and may move from place to place and/or job to job. As a result, we often have trouble manifesting what we want in life. Financial problems may arise due to poor management of resources. We may have excessive health problems or an unhealthy diet.

Earth-dominant people can be stubborn and resistant to change. We can be dull and preoccupied with mundane life. We can also be very materialistic, which manifests in behaviors such as greed, hoarding, and, if we lack resources, theft. Preoccupation with material matters may lead us to neglect the spiritual and intuitive aspects of our lives.

Spirit is the life force, the source of consciousness. It plays a unique role in the elemental model in that spirit serves to both separate and unite the other elements. Spirit gives us purpose in life, and spirit connects us with everything else. Baphomet is the egregore of the spirit of everything within the biosphere.

Due to the special role that spirit plays in regard to the other four elements, many religious and spiritual paradigms erroneously believe that spirit is superior to the material elements; their deities therefore reside in remote spiritual realms (often located in the sky above the inferior material world) and their representatives and followers are often required to separate themselves from material life to bring themselves closer to spirit. Erroneous beliefs about the superiority of spirit are one major factor that has contributed to our disconnection from the material four elements and the planet.

The truth is that spirit resides *within* the elements, not separate from them. Spirit works in synergy with the other four elements to create the biosphere that sustains us, and thus spirit exists within us and the biosphere around us.

When we're deficient in spirit, we often feel a lack of purpose in our lives. We may feel like we're just going through the motions, that nothing has any real meaning. We may also feel disconnected from the world and people around us.

Spirit-dominant folks often lose touch with reality—we're so busy basking in enlightenment or fervently pursuing our spiritual path that we forget to pay the bills or to engage in personal hygiene. We may consider ourselves superior to unenlightened people and treat them like children or idiots. We may appear to be spaced out or even insane, babbling about things that make little or no sense to other people.

The special relationship between spirit and the other elements can be expressed in two figures. The anthropomorphic (microcosmic) pentagram, with a human figure drawn within, places spirit at the topmost point in correspondence with the brain, the spiritual organ. The biospheric (macrocosmic) pentagram, with a goat's head within, places spirit at the lowest point to signify that spirit is within the four elements that make up the biosphere. Both pentagrams are inscribed within a circle to indicate that the elements are interconnected.

Upright and Inverted Pentagrams

Human physiology provides a good example of how the elements work together. Fire is associated with metabolism, which takes place primarily in the digestive system. Cellular metabolism is the main source of heat in the body. Water is associated with the circulatory system, with the blood that flows throughout the body distributing oxygen (air) and nutrients (fire / earth) to cells, and carrying away waste products. The blood also absorbs and redistributes heat produced by cellular metabolism. Air is associated with the respiratory system, which allows us to breathe, and the nervous system, which allows all parts of the body to communicate and coordinate. Earth is associated with the skeletal system, the stable framework of the body, and skin, the largest organ in the body, which contains and protects other parts of the body. Spirit is associated with the brain, which is the organ of consciousness and spiritual perception.

Exercise: Experiencing the Elements

The elements are all around us, so to work with individual elements simply requires that you use your will to concentrate and contain the energy of the element. Once this has been done, you can interact with the element and use the energy in magical operations.

1. Close your eyes and take a few deep breaths to clear your mind. Now visualize a transparent sphere in front of you, around two feet in diameter.
2. Say: "I call forth the energy of [element]." Visualize the sphere filling up with the energy of that element in the appropriate color. You may also visualize the sphere filling with the physical manifestation of the element, such as flames for fire or white light for spirit. However, remember that the elements consist of much more than their physical manifestations.
3. Hold the visualization in your mind for a minute while you consider the qualities of the energy before you. Then take your hand and put it into the sphere of elemental energy. What does it feel like on a physical, mental, and spiritual level? The elemental energy in the sphere will naturally connect with the elemental energy in your body. How does that make you feel?
4. When you are done interacting with the element, remove your hand. Feel the elemental energy of your body disconnecting from that of the sphere. Say: "I release this energy of [element]." Visualize the sphere containing the energy disappearing and the energy within being released back into the world. Ground yourself to release any excess energy.
5. Record your experiences in your journal.

I recommend working with each of the elements in this manner to familiarize yourself with their qualities and energies. Instructions on how to use these elemental spheres to balance your elemental makeup are given in chapter 12.

Exercise: The People in Your Elemental Neighborhood

One way to gain understanding of how the elements' qualities manifest in our own lives is to look at how they manifest in other people. Go through the descriptions of the elements above and think of people that possess or express those characteristics. You don't have to limit yourself to the real world—characters from books, TV, movies, and even video games can be used as examples. When you come upon multiple examples of a characteristic or dysfunction, compare and contrast them to see how they differ. This will help you understand the nuances between similar elemental expressions.

Another variation of this exercise is to choose someone you know really well and analyze their elemental composition. What elemental qualities do they have? Do they show any signs of being dominant or deficient in one or more elements? Record your observations in your journal.

Climate Change and the Elements

We aren't the only ones struggling with elemental imbalances. Climate change is also disturbing the elemental composition of the biosphere—of Baphomet. In fact, modern humanity's elemental imbalances are a direct cause of the elemental imbalances within the biosphere, which is why rebalancing our elemental composition is an important part of changing our relationship with the planet. We have forgotten that the microcosm (humanity) and the macrocosm (Baphomet) are interconnected, a fact represented in the upward and downward pointing arms of the Baphomet icon, commonly interpreted as symbolizing the Hermetic axiom "as above, so below." This is the result of our ignorance.

Air: Climate change is a phenomenon that occurs primarily in the realm of air. Human activity releases large amounts of carbon dioxide and methane into the air; these gases increase the temperature of the planet by trapping and reflecting heat rather than letting it dissipate into space. Increases in air temperature cause atmospheric phenomena to increase in intensity, resulting in more severe hurricanes, tornadoes, and storms.

Climate change can be a difficult concept for many people to grasp because like the air around us, it is mostly invisible. While it is true that sometimes pollution may be visible as smog or wildfire smoke, most of the time gases that contribute to the greenhouse effect are not visible to the human eye.

Fire: The gases that contribute to climate change come from burning. We burn fossil fuels for energy and burn forests to clear them for livestock grazing, which releases carbon dioxide. The metabolism of food by cattle and pigs raised for human consumption produces methane.

The primary effect of climate change is an increase in temperatures all over the world. As the world gets hotter, the detrimental effects of this heat on our biosphere become more pronounced. Many species of plants and animals, including humans, cannot adapt fast enough to cope with rising temperatures, which leads to suffering and death. By the end of the century, some areas of the world will become too hot for many creatures to survive, particularly those regions closest to the equator.

Earth: Plants use photosynthesis to turn carbon dioxide into nourishment and release oxygen as a by-product of the process. Humanity continues to clear forests to create more space for people, agriculture, and livestock grazing, which means that there are fewer plants to convert carbon dioxide to oxygen, depriving the biosphere of its ability to offset the increase of carbon dioxide in our atmosphere. Destruction of forest land also leads to a decrease in biodiversity by destroying the habitat that many plants and animals depend on for survival.

Water: Climate change disrupts the hydrological cycle, resulting in drought, severe rainstorms, and flooding. The ocean absorbs 90 percent of the heat generated by global warming, and dramatic increases in temperature kill fish and marine plants, especially coral beds. The ocean also absorbs around 30 percent of the carbon dioxide released into the atmosphere, leading to ocean acidification that also destroys marine life. Depletion of fresh water sources makes it more difficult for animals and humans to withstand increasing global temperatures. Melting glaciers and ice sheets combined with our dramatic increase of extraction of groundwater has actually caused a significant shift in Earth's axis of rotation. Rising sea levels will flood coastal communities and cause significant shoreline erosion.

Spirit: The spiritual result of climate change is a decrease in the planet's life energy. Climate change and the widespread destruction of natural habitats due to human activity have caused significant damage to the Earth's biosphere. This destruction directly affects Baphomet, the deity of the biosphere, who has come forth to change our destructive activities and restore planetary balance.

COAGULA
SOLVE

Chapter 12

Elemental Alchemy

The domination of the biosphere by humanity has led to serious environmental problems that have damaged the ecological balance of the planet. Three elemental factors have contributed to humanity's destruction of the planet:

1. Many humans have become disconnected from the five elements as they exist in nature.
2. Most humans suffer from elemental imbalances that have detrimental effects on their quality of life and distort their environmental decisions.
3. The results of human activity have created elemental imbalances on a global scale that threatens to damage and destroy life on this planet.

One of the first steps to combat climate change and ecological destruction is to reconnect with the elements and to balance the elements within us, a process called elemental alchemy. Elemental alchemy increases our environmental awareness, which will help us make better choices that will reduce the damage that we inflict upon the planet.

A well-balanced elemental composition also provides a good foundation to work from as we strive to change humanity's dysfunctional relationship with the earth.

Elemental alchemy is a three-step process. First, you must reconnect with the elements in the natural world; second, you assess your relationship with the elements; and third, you work to repair any significant elemental imbalances you uncover. It is important to reconnect with the natural elements before seeking to balance them within yourself, as it is more difficult to work with the elements when you are disconnected from them, and the process of reconnecting with the elements may help rectify some of your elemental imbalances.

Understand that there are many factors that can disconnect people from the elements or cause elemental imbalances that cannot be healed by elemental alchemy. Mental illness, psychotropic medications, and psychoactive drugs can negatively affect your elemental composition, and while elemental alchemy might alleviate some of the symptoms that result from these issues, it does not address the root cause of these problems like consulting a doctor, therapist, or drug counselor does. Likewise, elements of your shadow may cause elemental imbalances that can only be resolved through integrating parts of your shadow. However, elemental alchemy can still be a useful tool for discovering some of these factors as well as helping you heal them.

Elemental Disconnection

Modern society has disconnected us from the five elements.

For thousands of years, humanity had a much more intimate relationship with the elements. Fire was used to heat our dwellings, cook our food, and provide light after the sun went down. We had to live near sources of water needed for drinking, growing food, hydrating livestock, and transportation. People spent more time outside in the open air and sunlight. Dwellings were constructed from locally available materials. Our lack of knowledge about how things worked gave us a sense of wonder and awe that reinforced our spiritual connection with the planet.

Our lives still revolve around the five elements. Electricity has replaced fire as our primary sources of light and heat. Faucets and pipes provide water for hydration and cleansing. HVAC units circulate air though buildings and control the temperature within. The structures that we live and work in provide the stability and protection of elemental earth. Spirit manifests in the life present within our structures and is shaped by our experiences within.

The problem with modern living is that it separates us from the natural sources of the elements. Electricity is generated from many different sources, often a mixture of green technology like solar panels and wind farms and more polluting methods such as coal-powered generators. Fire-producing substances like oil and natural gas are extracted from the ground all over the world, then refined and transported to our homes. Our water usually comes from sources many miles away or far underground, running through long pipes to a treatment plant, then through many more long pipes to our homes. Indoor air is often separated from outdoor air and processed to be warmer or colder by modern devices. As for earth, very few people are involved in the construction of the buildings they live and work in, and the materials used in construction often come from many sources beyond our local area. Finally, modern buildings often separate us from the spirit of the natural world around us. Our buildings literally protect us from the elements, and many of the things that make modern life more secure and convenient also separate us from the natural elements.

Our separation from the elements of the natural world is the source of our physical, psychological, and spiritual suffering. This separation has also contributed to climate change that has had a devastating effect on our biosphere. Reconnection is the solution.

Reconnecting with the Elements

The first step in elemental alchemy is reconnecting with the elements in nature. This sounds very simple—just go out in the woods and everything will get better—but it is actually a little more complicated than that. We've put in a lot of effort to achieve and maintain the standards of modern living that have separated us from the elements. In turn, we will have to make a significant effort to go out into nature and reconnect with the elements. You need to do more than just walk down a trail and back—you need to stop and spend time truly connecting with nature, and you need to do it on a frequent basis.

Start by visiting a nearby forest or other natural habitat that is devoid of humans. Stop and take some time to observe the area around you. Here are some ideas to contemplate:

- Everything surrounding you is comprised of the five elements. Everything has spirit, and thus everything is connected to Baphomet; in this way, everything is connected to you. This is the essence of Baphometic consciousness—connection. Close your eyes and sense your connection to everything around you.
- Use all of your senses to explore the world around you (except taste—never taste or ingest anything you find out in the wilderness unless you can clearly identify it). Feel the bark on the trees, touch the water at the shore, smell the flowers, listen to the birds and the rustling of plants, etc.

- The evolution of natural habitat takes time. Consider the age of the things around you, such as the trees that tower above you that took many years to reach that height, and the dirt and rocks beneath your feet that are much older than the trees, and the fact that they are all much older than you.
- Where there is life, there is also death. Look for signs of death and decay like broken branches, fallen leaves, rotting logs, and animal carcasses. Consider that there are scavengers all around you, many of which you cannot see, such as ants, worms, and bacteria.
- Don't take anything from an area without asking for permission from the spirit of the place or from Baphomet. If you want something for your altar or a ritual, ask; otherwise, leave nature alone—we already take more than our share from the earth.
- Do take pictures and videos of your travels in nature so you can enjoy them later. Videos involving water, like streams, waterfalls, or ocean waves, can be especially calming and satisfying to revisit.

There are also many ways that you can connect with the elements in nature without travelling into the wilderness:

- Gardening and landscaping put us in touch with the cycles of nature and get our hands in the soil. If you can't plant things outside, bring plants into your home. Growing and caring for plants involves fire (sunlight and fertilizer), water, and earth (soil); plants transform air (photosynthesis) and possess spirit (life force).
- Go on an elemental walk. Choose an element, and, as you walk, look for evidence of qualities of that element in the

world around you. While air is invisible, you can observe it in the movement of trees and plants and of birds and insects, and you can feel it moving around you. Spirit is manifest as the life force of the multitude of living things around you both visible and invisible.

- Walk barefoot. Shoes and socks make walking more comfortable, but our ancestors spent a lot more time with their feet in actual contact with the earth. When the weather permits, spend some time outside in your yard or a park barefoot—it will help you connect with the earth. Finally, if you ever need to do some heavy-duty energy grounding, like after a traumatic event or intense magical operation, nothing works better than planting your bare feet on a patch of soil or dirt while you push the energy into the earth.
- If you lack the time or resources to get out into nature, use your computer. While watching videos indoors is not the best option for connecting with the outdoors, it can still be beneficial. Just looking at images of forests, deserts, and other natural habitats can relax us and remind us of our connection to nature. So can TV shows about the natural world and wild animals, which often have the added benefit of reminding us of the damage we have done to the earth and our responsibility to preserve natural habitat. Search for "natural sounds" on YouTube, and you can watch water rushing down a stream in the woods with birds chirping in the background or listen to ocean waves crashing on tropical shores. If you can't get outside, an internet connection can always bring the outside to you.

The amount of time needed to reconnect with the elements varies significantly from person to person. It is primarily dependent on the depth of your original connection to the elements. Your lifestyle is also a significant factor: an urban office worker is usually less connected to nature than a rural farmer. In any case, there is no test to determine the strength of your connection to the elements—it's something you have to assess for yourself. It is therefore recommended that you work on reconnection for at least a couple of weeks before attempting to assess your elemental imbalances, and that you continue to work on reconnection while rebalancing your elemental composition. Reconnection and rebalancing are synergistic processes—connecting with the elements in nature promotes internal elemental healing, and working with the elements within yourself will also strengthen your connection to the natural elements.

Assessing Elemental Imbalances

Each one of us has our own unique elemental composition that shapes who we are and how we interact with the world. Many people have natural affinities with certain elements. For example, some people are very empathic (water), while others are very energetic (fire), intellectual (air), grounded (earth), or spiritual. These elemental strengths are a healthy part of who we are. Thus the goal of balancing the elements is not to equalize the elements within us, which would remove our elemental strengths and destroy our unique nature, nor is there an ideal elemental combination for humans to aspire to in any case. The goal is to rectify the elemental imbalances that have detrimental effects on your life and happiness.

Our elemental composition is constantly in flux, reacting and adapting to internal and external stimuli, and temporary elemental imbalances are natural and even essential parts of life. For example, the loss of a loved one throws our elements out of balance. We become very emotional (water-dominant) and we often have trouble concentrating because our minds are trying to process the loss and what it means for our future (air-deficient). We may have lost a source of financial or emotional stability in our lives (earth-deficient), and often we cope with our grief by trying to stay busy (fire-dominant) or withdrawing from activities due to a lack of energy (fire-deficient). The event may even change our relationship with spirit: we might question our spirituality or find solace in it, and we often feel disconnected from the world. All these things are normal parts of the grieving process. Most of the time, our elements naturally rebalance themselves: we feel better and life gets back to a new normal. However, sometimes our reaction to these events leads to elemental imbalances that require intervention.

An elemental assessment will likely reveal that you are deficient in one or more elements and dominant in others. Personal elements may also be unbalanced themselves, fluctuating between deficient and dominant qualities. An assessment will also reveal your elemental strengths and natural affinities for elements, which, once known, can provide you with valuable stability and strength when working on rectifying imbalances.

There are many methods you can use to assess elemental imbalances. Self-assessment can be achieved by way of self-analysis and tools such as the tarot. You can also get advice and insight about your elemental composition from external sources, such as by talking to Baphomet or other deities, or even other spiritual entities. I encourage you to use whatever methods resonate most with you.

Exercise: Elemental Self-Analysis

This self-analysis exercise requires a significant amount of honesty and introspection to be truly effective. You can also have a friend, spiritual mentor, or other person that you trust assist you with this exercise—they are likely to see elemental qualities and issues that you are not aware of.

1. Read through the general description of each of the qualities of the elements given in chapter 11 and ask yourself two questions: What are the qualities of this element that I identify with? What qualities are lacking in my life? Make a list of both qualities in your journal.
2. Next, look at the descriptions of people with deficient or dominant elements (refer to "The People In Your Elemental Neighborhood" exercise on page 207). Do any of these qualities describe your relationship with the element? List them in your journal.
3. Go back through each of the items in your lists and write about why you possess or lack certain qualities. Meditate on the qualities that defy analysis.

Tarot

The structure of the tarot lends itself naturally to elemental work. The minor arcana consists of four suits that correspond to the four elements, while the major arcana consists of 22 trump cards that correspond to spirit. Occult tarot decks like the Thoth tarot deck work best for elemental workings because the numbered suit cards prominently display the elements in their iconography. Decks that use scenes to define the numbered cards, like the Rider-Waite-Smith, can still be used, but you may have to examine them a little deeper to understand their elemental connections. The Elemental Cross spread given below works more as a diagnostic tool than a divinatory one.

Exercise: The Elemental Cross Spread

1. To start, separate the deck into five piles, one for each of the four suits and one for the trumps.
2. State your intent: "In the name of Baphomet, I ask for insight on my personal elemental composition."
3. Shuffle each pile, draw three cards, and place them in the shape of a cross as shown in the following figure. (While ideally the vertical arms of the elemental cross might consist of three cards placed in a column, on the practical level this arrangement takes up too much space. The placement of the three cards in a row also encourages you to read them as a group rather than as three separate cards.) Deal the trump cards first; you may deal the elemental cards in any order you see fit. In the Elemental Cross spread, elements are placed in the four directions according to the attributions used in ceremonial magick: earth (disks) in the north, air (swords) in the east, fire (wands) in the south, and water (cups) in the west. However, you may place the elemental sections in any direction that corresponds with your magical tradition.
4. Examine each of the elemental sections and ask yourself: "What do these cards tell me about my relationship to each element? Is my relationship with the element balanced or unbalanced? If it is unbalanced, is the element deficient or dominant in my life?"

   In this spread, court cards represent your outward expression of the element and/or how the element affects your relationship with others. Aces represent the purest form of the elements and generally indicate a well-balanced relationship with the elements. However, sometimes they indicate that you normally have a balanced relationship with the element, but not in situations indicated by other cards in the elemental arm. Sometimes the cards in the elemental sections will indicate the nature or reason for the imbalance.

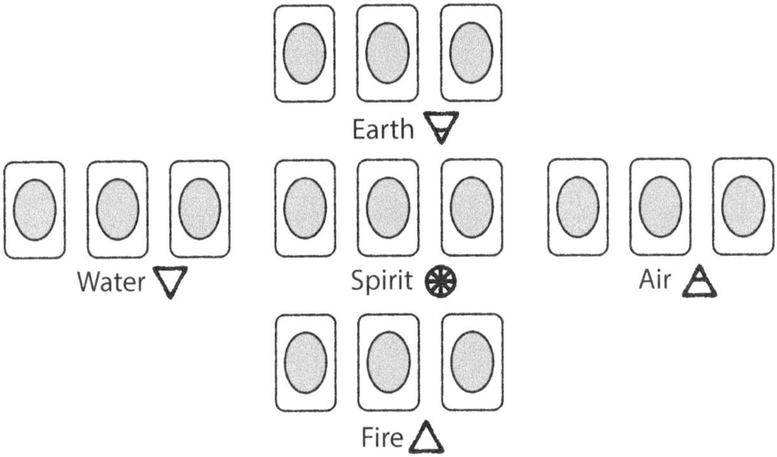

The Elemental Cross Spread

5. Examine the three trumps in the center and ask yourself: what do these cards tell me about my sense of purpose in my life? What do they tell me about my spiritual path and my relationship with spirit?
6. Examine the spread for patterns or relationships between the cards in the four elemental sections, and between the elemental cards and the trumps. These relationships can give you further insight into the nature of the elemental imbalances in your life. Finally, consider that some

dominant or deficient elements may contribute to other elemental imbalances.

7. Take a picture of the spread and record the results in your journal.

You can also use the Elemental Cross spread as a tool for self-assessment, in which you select the cards instead of choosing them randomly. Start by taking one elemental pile and spreading it out on the table in front of you in two rows of seven cards. Then select three cards that represent your relationship with that element; the order of the cards is not important and can even be changed during the course of the exercise. Repeat this process for the other three elements. Next lay out the trump cards by placing the Fool at the top and the numbered trumps in three rows of seven cards. Pick one card that represents you or your current spiritual situation in life and put it in the center, then select two more cards that represent significant issues or influences in your life and place them on either side. Once the spread is complete, examine it as discussed in steps 4 through 7 above.

Seeking Advice

If you're having trouble assessing your elemental imbalances, you can always ask for help. I recommend using the Wisdom of Baphomet meditation to ask Baphomet for assistance, for obvious reasons. Another option is to ask for help from a deity or another spiritual entity whom you trust. If you are a member of a temple, coven, or other magical group, you may ask other members for their opinions and advice.

Repairing Elemental Imbalances

There are many ways to repair elemental imbalances. The first step in the process to rebalance your elemental makeup is to ask Baphomet for help. Baphomet has come forth to initiate change in our lives and will offer valuable support and advice to those striving to achieve elemental balance.

Healing imbalances of spirit usually requires different methods than healing imbalances of the other four elements due to the special role that spirit plays in relation to the other elements. Those seeking to rectify imbalances of spirit should contact Baphomet and consult with Them on how to proceed. I'm not saying that you can't use the exercises in this book to work with spirit; I'm simply suggesting that you consult with Baphomet on the matter before you do. As the Spirit of the Earth, They can give you unique insight into your issues with spirit.

There are three strategies for rebalancing an element within yourself. First, you can use the energy of an external element to rebalance that same element; for example, you can work with fire to increase or decrease the fire energy within yourself. To increase fire within yourself, you would take energy from a source of fire; to decrease fire, you would give energy to a source of fire.

Second, you can use other elements to help you rebalance an element. Examples would be using earth to dampen and ground out excess fire energy or water to stimulate fire-based emotions to strengthen the fire within you. Remember that there are no opposite or gendered elements, so avoid those stereotypes.

Your third option is to find someone to help you with elemental rebalancing. While Baphomet is the obvious choice, you can also call on other deities and spiritual entities, especially those associated with the elements. Reiki practitioners and other people familiar with energy work can also assist you, as can other members of your spiritual community—don't neglect your human resources!

The following exercises can help you repair elemental imbalances. It is important to be patient when doing rebalancing work, as it usually takes a significant amount of time and effort to create lasting changes in your elemental composition. You must also give these exercises time to work; they don't necessarily have an immediate effect, and sometimes time is needed for your body to adapt to elemental changes. Avoid working with all of the elements in a short period of time, as it can put unnecessary stress on your energetic body. Meditation is a good way to check in with your body and determine when it's ready for more elemental work, but you can always ask Baphomet any questions about timing. The following exercise is a good way to start the rebalancing process.

Exercise: Elemental Baphomet Visualization

This visualization connects you with Baphomet so They can work on rebalancing your elemental composition. Baphomet will remove damaged, diseased, and unbalanced parts of your spiritual body and will energize and strengthen other parts. This can be an intense process, so I recommend that you set aside at least thirty minutes to perform this exercise and schedule some time to chill out after you're done.

1. Find a quiet and comfortable place to lie down.
2. State your intent: "Baphomet, I call upon you to transmute and balance the elements within me."
3. Close your eyes and visualize an image or statue of Baphomet. Feel the presence of Baphomet around you and within you.

4. Focus on the pentagram on their forehead; move closer to the pentagram until it dominates your vision. Then transfer the pentagram to your own forehead. Imagine the pentagram growing to enclose your body, with your head, arms, and legs extended in the points of the pentagram. Feel the energy of Baphomet flowing into the pentagram and manipulating the elements in your body. Pay attention to any images, sensations, or messages that arise from this exercise so you can record them later.
5. When Baphomet is finished, imagine the pentagram shrinking to rest on your brow. Open your eyes and thank Baphomet for helping you.
6. Record the experience in your journal.

Exercise: Elemental Immersion Therapy

One way to heal elemental imbalances is to immerse yourself in the elements in nature using the techniques described earlier in this chapter, in the section titled "Reconnecting with the Elements." Spending time in natural habitats has a balancing effect on our elemental composition. Natural phenomena can also be used to help you rebalance the elements within you using the Elemental Breathing exercise given below.

Exercise: Elemental Breathing

Elemental breathing is a visualization exercise that you can use to work with the elements. It employs the elemental spheres from the "Experiencing the Elements" section in the previous chapter, but you can also use it to work with other sources of elemental energy. For example, if you are near a physical manifestation of the element you wish to work with, such as a bonfire, the ocean, the wind, or a mountain, you can interact with these natural phenomena using this method. Or it may be more practical to draw from elemental sources that you can bring into your temple, such as a candle, salt, incense, or soil. Use whatever works best for you.

1. Close your eyes and visualize an elemental sphere filled with the element you wish to work with.
2. To increase a deficient element, inhale the energy of the element. Feel the energy enter your lungs and circulate throughout your body. Visualize the energy of the element in the appropriate color: Red for fire, blue for water, and so on. When you exhale, breathe out negative energy, visualizing it as a black smoke or vapor coming out of your body, out through your lungs, forming a cloud that quickly dissipates in the air.
3. To decrease a dominant element, inhale positive energy, visualizing it as white light or a white mist that circulates throughout your body. Next visualize the element within you, either in physical form or as elemental energy of the appropriate color. Breathe out the element, visualizing it leaving your body and being absorbed by the elemental source in front of you.
4. Repeat these breathing exercises for two minutes at first; once you have more experience with this process you may increase the time, or you can opt to continue this exercise until you feel that you have achieved the desired result. If at any point you feel either overly energized or depleted of energy, stop the exercise. When you are done, ground and center yourself.
5. Record your experiences in your journal.

Tarot

The Elemental Cross spread can help you identify ways to repair elemental imbalances. Before you start, state the purpose of the reading: "In the name of Baphomet, I ask for insight on how to balance the elements within me." Then deal the cards and interpret them normally.

You can also do a standard tarot reading using your preferred spread to investigate the causes of and solutions for particular elemental imbalances. You can start the reading with a general statement of intent such as, "Why am I water-deficient and what can I do about it?" or even ask more specific questions such as, "What can I do to become more empathic toward other people?" Take a picture of the spread and record your findings in your journal.

Magick

There are many Pagan traditions and magical systems that employ the elements. Wiccans call in the elements to energize and protect their magical circles. Ceremonial magicians use rituals like the Greater Ritual of the Pentagram and the Opening by Watchtower to do elemental work. Many other Pagan traditions have their own ways of working with the elements. If your magical tradition or group has rituals that work with the elements, you are welcome to use them to your advantage in the rebalancing process.

Another option is using sorcery to get advice from spiritual entities that rule the elements. Personally, I've received the best elemental advice from the elemental Archangels of ceremonial magic, Raphael (air), Gabriel (water), Michael (fire), and Auriel or Uriel (earth). I've also received elemental insights from the four Elemental Kings of the Enochian system, Bataivah (air), Raagiosl (water), Iczhihal (earth), and Eldprnaa (fire), and the Spirit of the Tablet of Spirit, EHNB. Many books provide instructions for calling forth these entities and speaking with them, including my own manual on sorcery, *The Complete Conjuring Spirits*.[170]

If you want to work without appealing to magical tradition or elemental rulers, you can use the Elemental Alchemy ritual given below to facilitate the rebalancing process. This ritual dispenses with the traditional temple equipment, pentagrams, and words of power used in other systems of magic. The elemental spheres used in previous exercises power this ritual, which turns your body into an instrument of the elements to create an elementally balanced circle.

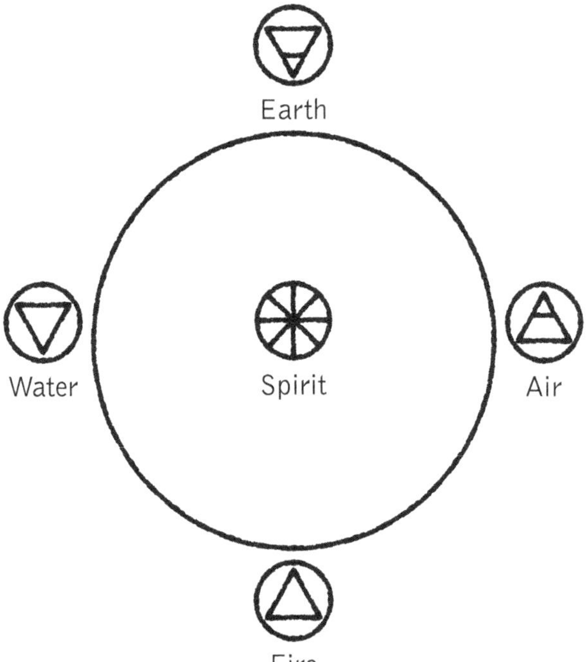

The Elemental Alchemy Ritual Circle

170. Michael Osiris Snuffin, *The Complete Conjuring Spirits* (Throned Eye Press, 2020).

A note on terminology: I use the term "sunwise" to designate the direction in which the sun travels through the sky. In the Northern Hemisphere, the sun travels clockwise, while in the Southern Hemisphere, the sun travels counterclockwise. The term "moonwise" refers to the opposite direction of sunwise, as the moon orbits Earth in a counterclockwise direction when viewed from the north pole and in a clockwise direction when observed at the south pole.

Elemental Alchemy Ritual

I. Opening the Circle

1. Stand in the center of your circle facing east.
2. Advance to the east. Visualize a yellow sphere of air energy in front of you. Say: "I call upon the element of air to aid me in purifying and consecrating this circle." Imagine the energy of air coming from the sphere and surrounding you in a halo of yellow light. Walk sunwise around the circle, carrying the energy of air with you. Return to the east. Say: "The energy of air is part of this circle." Imagine the halo of light returning to the yellow sphere.
3. Advance to the south. Visualize a red sphere of fire energy in front of you. Say: "I call upon the element of fire to aid me in purifying and consecrating this circle." Imagine the energy of fire coming from the sphere and surrounding you in a halo of red light. Walk sunwise around the circle, carrying the energy of fire with you. Return to the south. Say: "The energy of fire is part of this circle." Imagine the halo of light returning to the red sphere.
4. Advance to the west. Visualize a blue sphere of water energy in front of you. Say: "I call upon the element of water to aid me in purifying and consecrating this circle."

Imagine the energy of water coming from the sphere and surrounding you in a halo of blue light. Walk sunwise around the circle, carrying the energy of water with you. Return to the west. Say: "The energy of water is part of this circle." Imagine the halo of light returning to the blue sphere.

5. Advance to the north. Visualize a green sphere of earth energy in front of you. Say: "I call upon the element of earth to aid me in purifying and consecrating this circle." Imagine the energy of earth coming from the sphere and surrounding you in a halo of green light. Walk sunwise around the circle, carrying the energy of earth with you. Return to the north. Say: "The energy of earth is part of this circle." Imagine the halo of light returning to the green sphere.
6. Return to the center, the place of spirit, facing east. Visualize a halo of white light surrounding you. Say: "I call upon the element of spirit, which binds and separates the elements, to aid me in purifying and consecrating this circle." Advance to the east, then move around the circle sunwise three times, once for the earth, once for the sun, and once for the moon. Return to the center. Say: "The energy of spirit is part of this circle." Assume the attitude of Baphomet: raise your right arm with two fingers pointing up and extend your left arm toward the earth with two fingers pointing down. Say: "In name of Baphomet the Transmuter, this circle of the elements is now complete."

II. Working with the Elements

1. Feel the elements in perfect balance around you and bask in this sensation. Standing at the point of elemental balance will have a sympathetic effect on your own elemental composition.
2. To work with the four material elements, advance to the corresponding direction in your circle. Use the Elemental Breathing exercise above to exchange energy with the elemental sphere. Or you may use your own method of working with the elements. When you are done, return to the center of the circle.

III. Closing the Circle

1. Standing in the center of the circle, visualize a halo of white light surrounding you and say, "I call upon the element of spirit to aid me in releasing the elemental energies of this circle." Advance to the east, then move around the circle moonwise three times, once for the Sun, once for the Moon, and once for the Earth. Visualize the energy of the elements dispersing into the biosphere as you move. Return to the center and say: "This circle is closed." Let the energy of spirit surrounding you disperse or absorb it into your body if you so desire. Ground yourself.
2. Record the results in your journal.

You can use the opening and closing of the Elemental Alchemy ritual for any magical operations that involve working with Baphomet or the elements.

SOLVE
COAGULA

Conclusion

This book is meant to be a starting point—it gives you an idea of who Baphomet is and how to work with Them. However, there is still much more to be discovered about this deity, and I hope that this book will inspire others to add to the esoteric Baphomet corpus. I also hope that someday I will have the opportunity to issue a revised version of this book as more information about the deity Baphomet is revealed to me.

Working with Baphomet and performing elemental alchemy naturally inspires us to become more environmentally conscious. The realization that we are connected to everything in the biosphere can foster a deep desire to stop the destruction that threatens the planet. On a more experiential level, we can now see that climate change is already making our lives more difficult as we deal with the effects of heat, floods, droughts, wildfires, rising sea levels, and ocean acidification, and it's not going to get better anytime soon. Any way we look at the situation, we feel that we have a duty to do something about it.

One of the many books I discovered while researching this book was *Zen and the Art of the Saving the Planet* by Buddhist monk Thich Nhat Hanh, which includes a sobering yet enlightening meditation called the Five Remembrances:

> I am of the nature to grow old. There is no way to escape growing old.
>
> I am of the nature to have ill health. There is no way to escape having ill health.
>
> I am of the nature to die. There is no way to escape death.
>
> All that is dear to me and everyone I love is of the nature to change. There is no way to escape being separated from them.
>
> I inherit the results of my actions of body, speech, and mind. My actions are my continuation.[171]

I encourage you to contemplate these statements and gain whatever enlightenment you can from them. For me, the ultimate message here is that nothing in life is permanent except the results of our actions, and our actions in the near future will determine how much damage climate change will do to our planet and to our lives.

Like the three faces of Baphomet, we must strive to create change on three levels. The individual level is where we have the most power to create effective change by doing things like reducing our power and water consumption, recycling, driving less and/

---

171. Thich Nhat Hanh. *Zen and the Art of Saving the Planet,* ed. Sister True Dedication (Harper One, 2021), 46.

or using public transit more, and changing our diet. We have the power to create change in our local communities by promoting clean energy alternatives, restoring natural habitat, and teaching people (especially children) about climate change and the benefits of environmentalism. Finally, we can make a difference on a national or global level by joining national and international environmental groups like the Sierra Club, World Wildlife Fund, or Greenpeace; we can also educate politicians and business leaders about environmental concerns, lobby for stricter environmental laws and protections, and oppose efforts to expand fossil fuel production. This is just a partial list of actions we can take to improve our relationship with the planet; many more ideas can be found in books and on the internet. These actions may also serve as the most significant offerings to Baphomet.

Baphomet is the Spirit of the Earth, the egregore of the biosphere, the deity who has revealed Themselves unto us to influence us to change our way of living and stop the destruction of our planet. Their message is clear: we must make big changes now or we will be forced to make big changes in the near future. Now is the time to act.

COAGULA ET SOLVE

Bibliography

Addams, Ruth. *A Gift of Maggots: A Devotional for Baphomet*. Asphodel, 2010.

Andrews, Naomi J. *Socialism's Muse: Gender in the Intellectual Landscape of French Romantic Socialism*. Lexington Books, 2006.

Aquino, Michael A. *The Satanic Bible: 50th Anniversary ReVision*. Self-published, 2018.

Barber, Malcolm. *The Trial of the Templars* 2nd ed. Cambridge University Press, 2006.

Barber, Malcolm, and Keith Bate. *The Templars*. Manchester University Press, 2002.

Barruel, Augustin. *Memoirs Illustrating the History of Jacobinism*. American Council on Economics and Society, 1995.

Beck, Renee, and Sydney Barbara Metrick. *The Art of Ritual*. Celestial Arts, 1990.

The Blog of Baphomet: A Magickal Dialogue Between Nature and Culture. Accessed April 5, 2023. https://theblogofbaphomet.com.

Butler, Alan. *The Knights Templar: Their History and Myths Revealed*. Shelter Harbor Press, 2015.

Carroll, Peter J. *Epoch: The Esotericon & Portals of Chaos*. Illustrated by Matt Kaybryn. Arcanorum College, 2014.

———. *Liber Kaos*. Samuel Weiser, 1992.

———. *Liber Null & Psychonaut: An Introduction to Chaos Magic*. Samuel Weiser, 1987.

Chacornac, Paul. *Éliphas Lévi: Rénovateur de l'Occultisme en France*. N.P., 1926.

Church of Satan. "Welcome to the official website of the Church of Satan." Accessed April 5, 2023. https://www.churchofsatan.com/.

Constant, Alphonse Louis. *The Bible of Liberty*. Daath Gnosis, 2012. Originally published 1841 as *La Bible de la Liberte* by Le Gallois.

Cooper, Robert L. D. *The Red Triangle: A History of Anti-Masonry*. Lewis Masonic, 2011.

Crowley, Aleister. *The Book of Thoth*. Samuel Weiser, 1993.

———. *The Confessions of Aleister Crowley*. Edited by John Symonds and Kenneth Grant. Arkana, 1989.

———. *The Equinox* 1, no. 6. London, 1911.

———. *The Equinox* 3, no. 1. Detroit, 1919.

———. *Liber ABA, book 4, parts I–IV*. Samuel Weiser, 2000.

———. *Liber Aleph vel CXI: The Book of Wisdom or Folly*. Samuel Weiser, 1991.

———. *777 and Other Qabalistic Writings of Aleister Crowley*. Samuel Weiser, 1973.

———. *The Vision and the Voice with Commentary and Other Papers.* Samuel Weiser, 1998.

Dancyger, Lilly. "Satanic Temple Suing Netflix Over 'Sabrina' Statue Design" *Rolling Stone*, November 1, 2018. Accessed August 31, 2023. https://www.rollingstone.com/culture/culture-news/satanic-temple-suing-netflix-sabrina-statue-design-750868/.

DeHoyos, Arturo, and S. Brent Morris. *Is It True What They Say About Freemasonry?* M. Evans, 2010.

Drury, Neville. *The History of Magic in the Modern Age*. Carroll & Graf Publishers, 2000.

Endredy, James. *Ecoshamanism: Sacred Practices of Unity, Power & Earth Healing*. Llewellyn, 2005.

Ezzy, Douglas. *Sex, Death and Witchcraft: A Contemporary Pagan Festival*. Bloomsbury, 2014.

Hanh, Thich Nhat. *Zen and the Art of Saving the Planet*. Edited by Sister True Dedication. HarperOne, 2021.

Hawkins, Jaq D. *The Chaonomicon: Quintessential Chaos for the Serious Magician*. Goblin Publishing, 2017.

Hawthorn. "Baphomet 1999: Chaos, Controversy and Ecstasy." http://www.euphoriapagan.org/histories.html. Archived March 21, 2012. https://web.archive.org/web/20120321045235/http://www.euphoriapagan.org/histories.html#1999.

Herodotus, *The Histories*. Edited by John Marnicola. Translated by Aubrey de Sélincourt. Penguin, 2003.

Huson, Paul. *Mystical Origins of the Tarot: From Ancient Roots to Modern Usage*. Destiny Books, 2004.

IAO131. *HRILIU: Symbolic Explorations of the Gnostic Mass*. Self-published, 2016.

Kaczynski, Richard. *Perdurabo: The Life of Aleister Crowley*. North Atlantic Books, 2010.

———. *The Weiser Concise Guide to Aleister Crowley*. Red Wheel/Weiser, 2009.

Kaldera, Raven. *Dark Moon Rising: Pagan BDSM and the Ordeal Path*. Asphodel, 2006.

———. *Dealing with Deities: Practical Polytheistic Theology*. Asphodel, 2012.

———. *Hermaphrodeities: The Transgender Spirituality Workbook*. Asphodel, 2008.

Kaplan, Stuart R. *The Encyclopedia of Tarot, Vol. II*. U. S. Games Systems, 1986.

LaVey, Anton Szandor. *The Satanic Bible*. Avon, 1969.

Laycock, Joseph P. *Speak of the Devil*. Oxford, 2020.

Lévi, Éliphas. *The Book of Splendours*. Samuel Weiser, 1984.

———. *The Doctrine and Ritual of High Magic: A New Translation*. Translated by Mark Anthony Mikituk. TarcherPerigee, 2017.

———. *Fables et Symboles*. Germer-Baillière, 1865.

———. *The Great Secret, or Occultism Unveiled*. Samuel Weiser, 2000. Originally published 1898 as *Le Grand Arcane ou l'Occultisme Dévoilé* by Chamuel.

———. *Histoire de la Magie*. Germer-Baillière, 1860.

———. *The History of Magic*. Translated by Arthur Edward Waite. Samuel Weiser, 2001. Originally published 1859 by Rider & Co.

———. *The Key of the Mysteries*. Translated by Aleister Crowley. Samuel Weiser, 2002. Originally published 1861 as *La Clef des*

Grands Mystères Suivant Hénoch, Abraham, Hermès Trismégiste et Salomon by Germer-Baillière.

Lévi, Éliphas. *The Mysteries of Magic*. Edited and translated by Arthur Edward Waite. University, 1974. Originally published 1885 by George Redway.

———. *Transcendental Magic: Its Doctrine and Ritual*. Translated by Arthur Edward Waite. Samuel Weiser, 1999. Originally published 1923 by William Rider & Son.

Lovelock, James. *The Revenge of Gaia: Earth's Climate Crisis & the Fate of Humanity*. Basic Books, 2006.

McIntosh, Christopher. *Éliphas Lévi and the French Occult Revival*. State University of New York, 2011.

Nelles, David, and Christian Serrer. *This is Climate Change: A Visual Guide to the Facts*. The Experiment, 2018.

Paneque, Cosette. "Column: Australia's Pagan Festivals." *The Wild Hunt* (blog), November 14, 2015. https://wildhunt.org/2015/11/column-australias-pagan-festivals.html.

Papus (Gérard Encausse). *The Tarot of the Bohemians*. Translated by A. P. Morton. Senate Publishing, 1994. Originally published 1896 by George Redway.

Parry, D. L. L., and Pierre Gerard. *France Since 1800*. Oxford University Press, 2002.

Partner, Peter. *The Knights Templar and Their Myth*. Destiny Books, 1990.

Rachel. "Impressions of a first timer, Euphoria 2005." http://www.euphoriapagan.org/histories.html. Archived March 21, 2012. https://web.archive.org/web/20120321045235/http://www.euphoriapagan.org/histories.html#1999.

Rivera, Geraldo. *Devil Worship: Exposing Satan's Underground.* NBC/Universal Television. Originally broadcast October 22, 1988. Accessed April 6, 2023. https://www.youtube.com/watch?v=_71eQYY1Ncw.

Robinson, John J. *Born in Blood: The Lost Secret of Freemasonry.* M. Evans & Company, 1989.

The Satanic Temple website. https://thesatanictemple.com/pages/about-us. Accessed October 1, 2023.

Shelia. "An Interview with Seline." http://www.faunaliafestival.com/interview—seline.html.

Starhawk. *The Earth Path: Grounding Your Spirit in the Rhythms of Nature.* HarperOne, 2004.

Strube, Julian. "The 'Baphomet' of Éliphas Lévi: Its Meaning and Historical Context." *Correspondences* 4 (2016): 37–79.

Sutin, Lawrence. *Do What Thou Wilt: A Life of Aleister Crowley.* St. Martin's Press, 2000.

Uzzel, Robert L. *Éliphas Lévi and the Kabbalah.* Cornerstone, 2006.

Van Lujik, Ruben. *Children of Lucifer: The Origins of Modern Religious Satanism.* Oxford University Press, 2016.

Vayne, Julian, and Steve Dee. *Chaos Craft: The Wheel of the Year in Eight Colours.* The Universe Machine, 2016.

Waite, Arthur Edward. *Devil Worship in France, with Diana Vaughan and the Question of Modern Palladism.* Weiser Books, 2003. Originally published 1896 by George Redway.

———. *The Pictorial Key to the Tarot.* Causeway Books, 1973. Originally published 1911 by William Rider & Son.

Wasserman, James. *An Illustrated History of the Knights Templar.* Destiny Books, 2006.

Williams, Thomas A. *Éliphas Lévi: Master of the Cabala, the Tarot and the Secret Doctrines*. Venture, 2003.

Wirth, Oswald. *The Tarot of the Magicians*. Samuel Weiser, 1985.

Wyrd, Nikki, and Julian Vayne. *The Book of Baphomet*. Mandrake, 2012.

Art Credits

Interior illustrations:

Baphomet on pages xiv, 228. Illustration by Tim Foley.

Baphomet on pages x, 22, 176. Illustration by Éliphas Lévi, *Dogme et Rituel de la Haute Magie,* volume 2, 1856. Public domain. Digital image created by Erico Luxero. Attribution-Shareholder 2.0 Generic license. https://www.flickr.com/photos/olaechea/2920870064/.

Illustrations on pages 6, 8, 34, 50, 83, 94, 102, 105, 110, 128, 144, 168, 180, 194, 201, 206, 217, 224 by Rordan Brasington, Llewellyn Art Department.

Advertisement for Leo Taxil's *The Mysteries of Freemasonry Unveiled* on page 19. 1887 Created by Leo Taxil. Repository: Bibliothèque nationale de France. Rights reserved. https://gallica.bnf.fr/ark:/12148/btv1b9014879z.r=Taxil%2C%20L%C3%A9o?rk=150215;2#.

The Androgyne of Khunrath on page 33. Created by Heinrich Khunrath, *Amphitheatrum sapientiæ æternæ, solius veræ,* page 46, 1595. Repository: The University of Wisconsin–Madison. Libraries. Department of Special Collections. Creative Commons License. https://search.library.wisc.edu/digital/AH6PQ2FLXSD5FI8O.

The Devil Trump from the Marseilles Tarot on pages 53, 62. Tarot of Marseille. C. Burdel Schaffhouse, 1751. Used with permission of Lo Scarabeo.

The Devil Trump from the Rider-Waite-Smith Tarot on pages 57, 62. Tarot Original 1909 Deck © 2021 with art created by Pamela Colman Smith. Used with permission of Lo Scarabeo.

The Devil card from the Thoth Tarot on pages 62, 77. Copyright © Ordo Templi Orientis. All rights reserved. Thoth Tarot is a trademark of Ordo Templi Orientis.

Aleister Crowley as Baphomet X°, O.T.O. on page 65. Photograph by Arnold Genthe, *Equinox* 3, vol. 1. Universal Publishing Company, page 197, 1919. Public Domain Creative Commons. https://commons.wikimedia.org/wiki/File:Aleister_Crowley_as_Baphomet_X%C2%B0_O.T.O.jpg.

The Spell IV on page 80. Created by H.R. Giger. 1977. © Giger Estate.

To Write to the Author

If you wish to contact the author or would like more information about this book, please write to the author in care of Llewellyn Worldwide Ltd. and we will forward your request. Both the author and publisher appreciate hearing from you and learning of your enjoyment of this book and how it has helped you. Llewellyn Worldwide Ltd. cannot guarantee that every letter written to the author can be answered, but all will be forwarded. Please write to:

Michael Osiris Snuffin
℅ Llewellyn Worldwide
2143 Wooddale Drive
Woodbury, MN 55125-2989

Please enclose a self-addressed stamped envelope for reply, or $1.00 to cover costs. If outside the U.S.A., enclose an international postal reply coupon.

Many of Llewellyn's authors have websites with additional information and resources. For more information, please visit our website at http://www.llewellyn.com